Running with Walker

of related interest

Asperger's Syndrome
A Guide for Parents and Professionals
Tony Attwood
ISBN 1 85302 577 1

A Different Kind of Boy
A Father's Memoir About Raising a Gifted Child with Autism
Daniel Mont
ISBN 1 85310 715 5

Snapshots of Autism
A Family Album
Jennifer Overton
ISBN 1 84310 723 6

Autistic Thinking – This is the Title
Peter Vermeulen
ISBN 1 85302 995 5

From Thoughts to Obsessions
Obsessive Compulsive Disorder in Children and Adolescents
Per Hove Thomsen
ISBN 1 85302 721 9

Running With Walker

A Memoir

Robert Hughes

Jessica Kingsley Publishers
London and New York

First published in the United Kingdom in 2003
by Jessica Kingsley Publishers Ltd
116 Pentonville Road
London N1 9JB, England
and
29 West 35th Street, 10th fl.
New York, NY 10001–2299, USA

www.jkp.com
Second impression 2003
Third impression 2004

Library of Congress Cataloging in Publication Data
A CIP catalog record for this book is available from the Library of Congress

British Library Cataloguing in Publication Data
A CIP catalogue record for this book is available from the British Library

ISBN 1 84310 755 4

Printed and Bound in Great Britain by
Athenaeum Press, Gateshead, Tyne and Wear

Those who have been put aside and so often despised, or not seen as whole, when one becomes their friend, in some mysterious way, they heal us.

Jean Vanier

To David R. Hughes,
for his wit and courage

Contents

Prologue   Christmas Party, 1997   9

Chapter 1   A New Cult   21

Chapter 2   "Denial"   31

Chapter 3   Brothers   44

Chapter 4   Yes and No   54

Chapter 5   Child Development to the Rescue   65

Chapter 6   Homeschooling I: Cemetery School   83

Chapter 7   Homeschooling II: Running With Walker   96

Chapter 8   The Two Walkers   109

Chapter 9   "Nothing is Written"   121

Chapter 10   Maureen   134

Chapter 11   Yearning   148

Chapter 12   The Apocalypse   163

Chapter 13   Davy Crashes   179

Chapter 14   Liftoff?   192

Chapter 15   Apocalypse, Again   208

Chapter 16   Hope   223

Epilogue   June 2001   233

Christmas Party, 1997

"Ooooo, *baby!* It's a big old goofy *world!*"

The words hit my ears like an air raid siren. I flinch, duck, and look up, but too late. A Hot Wheels fire engine—a metal toy truck about three inches long—comes flying over the balcony above my head, hits the wall, ricochets off a supporting beam and *bang!* lands on the stove, right next to the mulled cider I'm stirring for the Christmas party. I dash out of the kitchen and up the stairs, three at a time, to the balcony bedroom and launchpad that overlooks our kitchen.

Walker, my twelve-year-old autistic son, is in the corner of the room bouncing wildly on a large inflated therapy ball, another Hot Wheels fire truck in his hand. He is still shouting the same line from a John Prine song even though to his right a tape player is blaring "Jingle Bell Rock" and to his left the video of "The Muppet Christmas Carol" is playing on a television set. His ten-year-old brother, Davy, oblivious to the racket, is perched on a high stool only a couple of feet away and coolly playing a video game on yet another TV set.

Taking my stand in the middle of all this fun technology, I shout, "What are you doing? You've got to settle down and relax!" I model the concept "relax" by frantically waving a wooden spoon in the air. "The guests are coming any minute now!"

"Ooooo, *baby!*" he yells again, looking very pleased.

"Say you're sorry for throwing the truck, Walker. Say you won't do it again."

"Take it easy, Dad," offers Davy without taking his eyes off his game. "He's just excited."

Walker smiles and says, "Sorry, Dad."

I force a near grin, give him a hug, take a deep breath, and make an effort to de-escalate my rising tension.

Walker looks terrific. A snapshot of him right now would show a tall, gorgeous, dark-eyed boy with glossy hair and a killer smile. Trim, square-shouldered, with graceful posture and a certain indefinable air of elegance, he seems like one of life's natural winners. In his turtle-neck black shirt and jeans, he's like a child model in a Gap ad.

A videotape of him, however, would reveal a very different boy. He sits and bounces on his giant inflated ball a little *too* high and *too* tire-lessly. He shouts words and phrases unconnected to the two things he's doing simultaneously—watching a video and listening to music. At unpredictable moments, he leaps up and rewinds parts of both his videotape and his audiotape. Much more rarely, he sends a little Hot Wheels missile into the air and gets some entertaining response from his father. He sometimes spits, loudly and vigorously and inelegantly, into a plastic bucket placed nearby. And he reacts to certain scenes in the video or lines in the songs or things Davy says by putting his fingers in his ears, blushing, curling up and staring at the floor.

As I walk down the stairs, I hear another "Ooooo, *baby!*" and stop. This time no follow-up smart bomb comes zinging by my head, so I keep walking.

I have good reason to worry. A half hour ago I gave Walker one milligram of Risperdal, a strong mood-controlling drug, just to help him remain calm enough to get through the party without some small cataclysm. But once again his astonishing energy seems to be powering right through any effect of the medication.

My wife, Ellen, and I know that Walker has it in him to stop the party dead. He could, if he loses control, start a virtual blitzkrieg—of Hot Wheels cars, audiotapes, videotapes, empty Coke cans, blankets, silverware, shoes, fistfuls of spaghetti—raining down on the guests from over the balcony into the living room and kitchen. These objects would be selected with cost and safety concerns in mind—for instance, he has never actually hurt anyone with a flying object, has never broken a window or thrown a TV or a table over the side—but his attention to safety is unlikely to be appreciated by every single guest. And stopping the party wouldn't require anything so flamboyant. Walker could simply start yelling an impossible request like "Waa waa school bus now!" (that is, "I want to ride in the school bus right now!") incessantly enough and loudly enough until self-consciousness drives everybody out of the house.

Most importantly, I, Dad, the nervous member of the family, would be fatally embarrassed. About sixty people are coming, and this party is only the second time since Walker's birth that we've tried to put on an event of this magnitude and exposed our little household on this scale. It's true that nearly all of those invited know something about Walker and probably expect to see some weird antics. But few know about the extremes to which Walker can go, the physicality and rage and frustration he can exhibit when he feels too lost and hopeless.

What I try to avoid thinking about is that Walker himself would feel crushed if he loses his fragile grip on his emotions. He adores Christmas, plays Christmas carols on his tape player year round, looks radiant at the mere mention of the tree, and snow, and Santa Claus. He has looked forward to this party for weeks, but he knows better than anybody that the excitement might be too much for him. For Davy, the main architect and planner of the event, a Walker party stoppage would be utter humiliation.

It's three o'clock on this Sunday afternoon near Christmas and time for the most literal-minded invitation readers to arrive. Right now Ellen is busy trying to do the impossible: straighten the porch room at the back of our small house, a room that quadruples as laundry room, office, random junk storage area, and main hangout for our three cats. I stand near the front window and look out and try to imagine what it would be like for unsuspecting guests, say a couple from the suburbs, to come to our house.

The first thing they would notice is that there is absolutely nowhere to park. Our house is in a North Side Chicago neighborhood that is so hip, so jammed with restaurants and live theater and shops and Jeep Wranglers and SUVs that a parking space is a small news event. A common remark spoken by someone who walks in our door, a remark made in a barely-disguised accusatory tone of voice is, "Wow! Heh, heh! I had to circle this block for twenty-five minutes!"

I imagine this unsuspecting couple having to park nearby on Belmont Avenue and walking in a state of alarm past a jarring variety of commercial establishments: a Starbuck's, a cigar shop, a Dunkin' Donuts, a sexual appliance emporium, a tattoo parlor, a transient hotel, a popular Swedish restaurant, an upscale women's clothing shop, and a store that specializes in large plaster gargoyles. They'd also pass a stunning range of city sidewalk types: from the evidently well-off to the obviously poor; from the spiky-haired, leather-jacketed, multiply body-pierced young person to the very stationary, very scary-looking guy. This poor man's Greenwich Village aspect of our neighborhood has been a quiet boon to us: Walker's startlingly odd outdoor behavior hardly rates a second look.

I try to convince myself, as I stand looking out the window, that this couple would be mollified and impressed when they finally get to our small two-flat house, lit up as it is by bright Christmas lights. After walking up the stairs and in the door, they would step into the cozy living room of a recognizably normal family. There's a fireplace on the right with a wood fire burning more or less successfully. There's a nicely-decked-out table with wine, a smoked ham, cookies, and home-baked bread on the left. And straight ahead there's a nine-foot Christmas tree, decorated within an inch of its life, that reaches up towards the high arched ceiling. The room is small, much too small for sixty guests, but I flatter myself that it's also pleasant and warm and seems like it was made for a Christmas party.

But doubts creep in. The walls, for instance. What if this couple takes a good look at them? Certain key spots—the banister along the stairs, the walls in three corners of the house and along the hallway, the ceiling near the back door, the whole area around the computer in the back room—have been permanently penetrated by Diet Coke, peanut butter, Kraft Spirals, pizza sauce, and other indelible delicacies. Walker is always touching the surfaces around him, either jumping in place at one of his stations, such as a corner, or dashing along a route, like the hallway and up the stairs. Keeping up with him would require fleet-footed, round-the-clock, obsessed janitorial personnel.

What if this couple silently catches on to our apparently loony financial priorities? The kitchen cabinets are missing two doors and the stairs up to the parents' bedroom are bare pine boards, but we have a startling array of electronic toys and an overwhelming library of kid videotapes. The ceiling of the back porch room is spotted by big water marks and loose plaster from a perpetually leaky roof, but it looms directly over an up-to-date computer, modem, scanner and printer. The screens on most of the windows are ripped, but there are stacks of expensive books hidden in all sorts of places. Certain tables and chairs will collapse if pushed at the wrong angle, but somehow we manage to afford a big supply of firewood. And there are strange little indentations, actually the five-year-old Walker's tiny teeth marks, studding the edges of tables and the banister and the corners of walls.

I want to, but won't, make an announcement in the middle of the party: "Attention! Attention, please! I know what you're thinking! But it is not financially sensible to replace things that (a) you can't afford to replace, and that (b) are only likely to be damaged again. Really! Thank you! Enjoy!"

Social self-consciousness is a stalker I seldom shake off. Ellen, much better at evading the feeling, comes into the room and offers me a glass of wine. "I know what you're doing," she says. "You're looking at the walls again. Take it easy. What's the worst that can happen?"

I smile at her little joke. We both know what can happen.

TWO HOURS LATER, to my surprise, all seems to be going well. Ellen is mixing, Bing Crosby is singing on the stereo, people are bumping elbows pleasantly; and I, working on my third glass of wine, am reasonably calm but wary as I chat with my friend and colleague,

George, in the kitchen. George and I teach English as a second language and freshman composition at the same City College in Chicago, and both of us went to graduate school in literature at Northwestern. This means that there are great piles of information in our skulls that we never have an excuse to show off except in conversations like this. I am about to stun George with a tidbit from my stash of useless knowledge when I hear an ominous shout overhead: "SPA-GHET-*TI*!"

This is not good. I brought a big bowl of spaghetti up to Walker about twenty minutes ago and have no more of it prepared, so I excuse myself and bound up the stairs to see what I can do.

Walker has never moved from his station in the corner where he has been bouncing on his ball, watching and rewinding "Muppet Christmas Carol," and holding court. Various guests, one by one, have come up here and greeted him. The more confident ones give him a hug and try out a little unilateral conversation on him, Groucho-to-Harpo style, the kind Ellen and I often ply him with:

"Oh, Walker, I see you're watching "Muppet Christmas Carol."

Walker gets up from bouncing on his ball and looks at the TV screen.

"I like that movie a lot. Do you like it?"

Walker smiles broadly and looks into the eyes of his visitor from just a few inches away.

"Yeah, it's great, and really funny. That Ratso sure is silly. But poor Mr. Scrooge!"

Walker looks at the screen and puts his fingers in his ears.

"He's really having a bad night, isn't he? Hey, there's the Ghost of Christmas Past. She's pretty, like a little fairy, isn't she?"

Walker, still smiling, sits down on the ball, fingers in ears, and stares at the floor.

"Conversing" like this can be hard work, but right now Walker's friend, Valerie, a skilled practitioner, is whispering something to him and trying to calm him down. As he sits quietly on his ball, she is on her knees next to him with her arm around his neck, both their heads bowed. Valerie is a cashier at the vast supermarket where Walker and I do most of the family's grocery shopping, and she has not only seen

Walker in action but helped to hustle us quickly through the line during some of his wilder outbursts.

Valerie looks up at me, smiles, and says, "I *think* he wants more spaghetti. I could be wrong, though."

"Right!" I say. "Walker, you take it easy while I make more spaghetti."

Walker has never actually held a "conversation," in the sense of a prolonged exchange, with anyone. As a "low-functioning autistic" (though this and other labels have proved to be of very little help in understanding him), he has extremely poor verbal skills. He speaks to others mainly in single words and phrases, many of which can't be understood. To our delight, however, he increasingly shouts long, incomprehensible sentences. We take this as a good sign. Autism is widely assumed to be an ineradicable disability, but Ellen and I, in our own shaky but resolute way, have never accepted this.

As I start to boil his spaghetti noodles, I listen for another shouted entrée request from above and wonder if he can make it all the way through the party without escalating further.

Christmas party nerves call up my own personal Ghost of Christmas Past.

Two years ago, on Christmas Eve, the four of us plus Ellen's mother, Phyllis, folded ourselves into our Escort and drove for an hour and a half out to the suburbs to my sister's annual party. Walker skipped happily up the driveway, ran in the door, yelled "Merry Christmas!", couldn't think of anything else to do, and after about a half hour went to the front door and started jumping up and down, screaming "GO HOOOM!" over and over. Going home was not an option; Davy would be crushed to have to turn around and leave, for he seldom had an opportunity to see his cousins and aunts and uncles. And Phyllis had only met my family once before, at our wedding. After about twenty minutes of nearly everyone trying to distract him and help him, I took him out to our car in the driveway.

The two of us sat in the front seat, and I tried to entertain him with Coke and crackers and the radio. A station was playing one of Lionel Barrymore's 1940s performances as Scrooge, and I pressed a one-way discussion of it on him. Walker would have none of it. He kicked the dashboard, grabbed me by the collar of my coat, tried to bite me, and shouted, "Go home!" over and over. So a grim routine began. I'd sit in the car and try to talk to him until I started yelling too. Then I'd step out of the car, close the door, and pace around in the snow. He'd look at me through the windshield, tears in eyes, shouting "Hoooome!" Then I'd wallow in self-pity for a while until I re-discovered enough mature parenting brain cells to talk to him calmly again. After a while Ellen would come out and spell me, and I would go in and pretend to celebrate. Though we knew Walker wanted to be there and was thrilled to see his family, he was too sad or frustrated, too angry or strangely panicked to handle it.

The stress of moments such as this is never equal to the sum of the inconvenience and embarrassment of the situation. Anxiety—the grim companion, the Ghost of Christmas Yet to Come—always dominates moments of trouble, as if saying to Ellen and me, "Fools! You think this is bad? Just imagine the future!"

Other Christmases, by contrast, had been idyllic. Once, at age five, Walker choreographed an elaborate, inventive little dance to a recording of Nat King Cole Christmas songs and performed it for our friends, Mary and Joe, and their daughters, Kathleen and Jane. The girls—looking and sounding like visiting angels—sang "Sisters" from "White Christmas." Everybody, Walker especially, seemed to inhale comfort and joy on a grand scale. Ever since then, Walker has shown an interest in performing at Christmas time, and this year we've practiced "Winter Wonderland." When the timing seems right (when is it ever right?) he and I will sing it together. Kathleen and Jane, now gorgeous eighteen- and twenty-year-olds, are here, and Walker would like nothing better than to sing it for them.

I suddenly hear another ear-piercing crescendo from over my head: "Aaaah, aaah, *AAAAH!*", but I don't know what the trouble is. So I call the boiling spaghetti noodles done and hurry them up to him.

Walker is always driven to communicate in one way or another. Shouting, crying, leaping thunderously up and down in one spot, or pitching audiotapes over the side from his upstairs corner—all of it is communication. Sometimes Walker seems like a kidnap victim in a bad movie: He's locked in an attic and tied to a chair with duct tape over his mouth. He can hear the police—Ellen and me and our cohort of doctors, therapists, and teachers—downstairs looking for him, so he knocks over the chair, kicks over a lamp, and thumps with his feet on the floor. Unfortunately, the police are well-meaning but dim,

Davy, age 3 and Walker, 6

earnest but clueless. The victim is close, very close, but the police continually misidentify the signs he's trying to give them.

GUESTS ARE BEGINNING to leave, so it's now or never for the boys' performances. First Davy sings a song of his own composition, "The Six Relatives of Christmas," sung to the tune of "The Twelve Days of Christmas." It's genuinely hilarious and darkly comic, the kind of song Bart Simpson would write if he had Davy's gift for parody. The guests stand in a circle around him, laughing and especially enjoying his post-song show stopper, standing on his head for three minutes.

Then Walker and I come down from upstairs, I holding his left hand while he ducks his head, blushes, and holds his right index finger in his ear. I tug him over to the circle Davy created and we stand side by side and do a pretty good job with "Winter Wonderland." My Andy Williams-style outstretched arms finale, I think, more than makes up for the fact that I forget the lines and mix up the verses slightly. The beaming presence of Kathleen and Jane and the hearty applause make Walker glow with pleasure and he dashes back up the stairs.

I breathe a sigh of relief. The party has been our family's version of total success.

LATER, AFTER THE guests have gone, the boys are in their beds in the bedroom they share. Ellen has gotten them into their pajamas and tucked them in and I go in to say good night.

Davy is sitting up reading a collection of "Calvin and Hobbes" comic strips. He finds Calvin soothing to read about, for he knows Calvin is a little like him: a lonely, sweet, misunderstood boy with an active imagination and striking intelligence. Davy has about a dozen stuffed animals tucked in around him, his favorite cat, Louis, asleep on his feet, and a stack of books next to his bed (among them, Edith Hamilton's *Mythology* and a couple of volumes of the encyclopedia). I kiss him good night and go over and sit on Walker's bed.

We had such a great success singing earlier in the evening, I think we could sing another song together. So I begin: "The first Noel, the angel did…" I hold out my open palm toward him to complete the line.

"No *say* today!" he shouts.

I press on: "Was to certain poor shepherds in fields as they…"

"No *lay* today!" He then grins broadly, sits bolt upright, and a wild, let's-get-crazy look comes into his eyes.

"OK, Walker. It's time to settle down. Good night, man." I smile, give him a hug, kiss him, pat Davy on the head, and turn off the light, all in as matter-of-fact a way as I can muster.

After I close the door, I hear: "Ooooo, *baby!* It's a big old goofy *world!*"

I pause in the hall for a minute, but the Walker War Cry signifies nothing more this time than a token jerking of my chain.

ELLEN IS UPSTAIRS getting ready for a short winter's nap in the technology playroom that doubles only incidentally as our bedroom.

I close the fireplace doors, turn off the porch lights, and take one last look at the Christmas tree before turning it off too. Ellen and Davy put all the lights and ornaments on it, and they did a great job. There is the big globe ornament with hundreds of gold pins in it, meticulously made by Kathleen and Jane when they were little girls. There is my favorite one, a kind of anti-ornament, a gas station lit up by a light and covered in snow that loudly advertises Coca-Cola, given to me by a friend who knows about my over-fondness for the stuff. Another one, a wooden reindeer that dances when you pull a string, was given to us by a neighbor.

And I spot one of several "Baby's First Christmas, 1985" ornaments that friends gave us in honor of Walker, who had just been born on December 2 of that year. As I look this one over—a tiny blue cradle made of popsicle sticks—it occurs to me how little our friends know about us. Who among our guests here tonight could ever guess how difficult and risky our modest Christmas production has been? Our impression of a near-normal family this evening—with our smiles and our jokes and our shabby-but-cute Potemkin village décor—was so good, in my opinion, that our guests probably went away thinking, *Well, that was a nice party. Walker's an attractive and charming boy. What's all the fuss about?*

I would like to explain what the fuss is all about, to tell Walker's story in such a way that others can understand my fumbling replies—"Pretty good" or "Not so good" or "A little better"—to the daily question "How are things going?" I would like to tell the story so that people who have no acquaintance with autism can understand us better—and perhaps other families like ours as well—when we try to describe why we still hold out hope with so little solid evidence to go on.

Most important of all, I would like to tell Walker's story so that others can know him, and other children like him, as much, much more than the strange kid shouting and bouncing on a ball in the corner with his fingers in his ears; as much, much more than a victim whose every move and every thought is determined by something called autism.

To do this I have to go back to the time when we discovered that our perfect little boy had a problem, and when we had no inkling of the trouble the big old goofy world held in store for him…

ONE

A New Cult

In the film "The Miracle Worker," the moment when the parents realize that little Helen Keller is blind and deaf is a scene of gothic horror, a life-shattering event. When a lantern is waved above her face and the parents realize she is blind, the mother screams, and the cinematographer has a grand time playing with menacing shadows and eerily-lighted faces.

Before Walker came into our lives, this was my idea of the way it would be to discover a catastrophic problem in a child: it would hit like a sudden shock, a psychic electrocution.

Ellen and I, however, never had anything like the classic crack-of-doom, lantern-over-the-crib moment. In fact, far from suspecting that we faced a serious problem, we spent the first two years of his life living like happy members of a new child-worshipping cult.

The photograph albums from those days do a good job of portraying a household in the grip of a love affair between parents and child. Picture after picture shows a dream of a kid: a pink, round, healthy face glowing with joy and enthusiasm; dark eyes full of sparkle and expectation and looking directly at the camera; a big grin that once provoked a friend to say, "He'll charm your socks right off your feet."

One sequence of pictures, the kind that bores senseless the friends of new parents, shows Walker at one and a half running up and down the little hallway in our house playing basketball. He's wearing a diaper and a white T-shirt and his curly hair is plastered to his head from the sweat of his play. In the first picture he's running down the hall, away from the camera, carrying a bright plastic ball for a classic toddler lay-up. In the second, he's poised on the edge of the three-foot-high basket rim about to stuff the ball, NBA-style. In the final picture, he is already running back, the ball on its way to the floor.

The big tip-off that this is not a true professional with "fire in the belly", not someone in the competitive "zone" of the superstar, is that he is laughing in every picture and has at least one eye conspiratorially locked on the camera. Even caught in mid-stuff, he is smiling at the camera, something a professional waits to do until after the basket is made.

Clearly, though, the boy has one surpassing talent: the ability to make his parents feel like they're the funniest, nicest, most lovable people on the planet—walking miracles of parenting.

Walker, age 1½

Two more striking features of this sequence of pictures are the energy of the boy and, in the few pictures that feature them, the sleepiness of the parents. Our favorite picture shows Walker at about age one standing in his crib just as we enter his room in the morning. He is beaming at us with joy and big hopes for his day, a poster boy of happy toddlerhood, without a care in the world.

What the picture does not show is the sleeplessness in his parents' eyes, for nearly every night Walker awoke at one or two or three a.m., stood up in his crib, and bounced, rhythmically and loudly compressing the springs under his mattress—*skreek, skreek, skreek, skreek*—for a half hour, an hour, or an hour and a half, as Ellen and I lay awake, listening and whispering: Should we go down and tell him to go to sleep? Should we get him up and play with him? Should we ignore it? And worst of all, Should we sell the house and move? We had a tenant in the first floor apartment just below Walker, and we speculated constantly about whether our noise would drive him away.

The sleep problems, in retrospect, were a very early sign that something was wrong. But we chalked them up to the same native energy that propelled him around the house all day. He'd get up and dive into a pile of picture books and turn the pages with interest for an hour; then play with his train; then watch "Sesame Street" while hopping around and laughing; then sit in his highchair and cover his grinning face with food.

And always, always, he demanded the audience of Mom and Dad for everything he did, every move he took. Each little achievement had to be rewarded with a hug, every success capped off by burying his face in his mother's hair.

ONE EVENING OVER dinner our friend Christine, an elementary school teacher, let us in on a trade teacher joke. "There are only three kinds of children: Gifted, Very Gifted, and Severely Gifted." Ellen and I laughed but secretly thought the same thing: "Yes! 'Severely Gifted.' A category for Walker!"

We knew our two-year-old was severely active. His midnight crib aerobics made his mattress the first casualty in what would be a steady cycle of furniture depletion and renewal. Our house resembled a sort of brightly-colored, Fisher-Price livestock pen with chutes and gates to control the speeding, ricocheting, climbing, jumping, alarmingly robust kid. A long hike outside with Walker in his umbrella stroller was, even then, a pedestrian-stopping show, for even trapped in his seat, he was still on the move, rocking and waving his arms and smiling at everyone who passed.

Always in motion, he became a devotee of Fred Astaire. I made a video clip of Astaire doing his "Puttin' on the Ritz" number from the film "Blue Skies" and Walker was instantly mesmerized. He'd stand a foot away from the TV and imitate the steps, stop and stare open-mouthed and wide-eyed at Fred's feet, then resume, trying to get it right. He'd then move his act into the kitchen and stare at the reflection of moving feet in the window of the oven. At the end, every time, he'd turn to us for applause.

Like Fred Astaire, Walker loved to dance with a partner. Ellen would put on a Patsy Cline or Hank Williams or Emmylou Harris tape, pick him up, and spin around our bedroom with him. Walker's style was more like Gene Kelly's, however, physical and vigorous. He would lean back in Ellen's arms (the better to see his partner), lurch up and down in time with the music, and show such rapturous love of melody and movement, such sublime inelegant appreciation, that putting him down seemed cruel. So Ellen would pass him over to me, and I'd waltz around until I was staggering and pass him back to her. We were of the "Follow the Leader" school of parenting, and we had no doubt who our leader was.

We knew, too, that he was a severely loving little boy. When Ellen's mother, Phyllis, came for a visit, she would sit on the floor and shout "Fierce hugs!" Walker would grin, get a wild look in his eyes, run toward her with his arms stretched out, and the two of them would tumble over, hugging and kissing. When my brother Peter dropped by, Walker would grin up at him, jumping up and down as if Uncle Pete had come with the bail money. When my mother was able to visit from her home in Tennessee, he would snuggle into her arm and listen to her read stories.

But he was severely puzzling. He started saying his first words at a normal age, but at one and half the speaking started to trail off. Thereafter he entered upon a three-year period of almost complete silence, speeding around the house busily and happily but soundlessly. We knew he wasn't deaf—even our talented tiptoeing in the early morning wasn't enough to keep him from stirring. And he seemed to understand us—he laughed at little verbal jokes and responded knowingly to our talk in countless ways. But because he didn't speak, we were frequently left in the dark about what he knew and didn't know, a condition that would grow into maddening proportions as time went by.

Compounding the mystery was the fact that he wouldn't play with toys in an expected way. Someone got him one of those toys you push with a stick and goes "pop pop pop pop" across the floor. I enjoyed it myself well enough, marching around the house and showing him how the big guys do it, but Walker never pushed it at all. Some toys he'd play with in a sort of marvelous way, but others, especially ones that demanded physical assertiveness—pushing, punching, pulling—he'd avoid.

In the marvelous category were what Ellen and I referred to as his "Plastic Pals." These were five brightly-colored, foot-tall zoo animals on wheels who traveled with him throughout the house. They were busy fellows who had big plans and were often called upon to speak into a toy telephone, have their hearts checked with a toy stethoscope, and line up in a caravan for long trips. They were Walker's children, for he pretty much treated them as we did him: he even silently "read" his books to them. Mom and Dad were constantly enlisted to speak to them, discuss their health, and praise their accomplishments. Walker put on little dramas with them and called on them to observe his activities, positioning them so they could "watch" him play. But all this stage managing and directing was done wordlessly, with animated gestures and happy smiles; he was Harpo, strangely content to let Groucho and Chico, Ellen and me, do all the talking.

Against the backdrop of his lack of speech and sometimes odd play, Walker's flat-out giftedness came as a relief and a surprise, revealing itself in one of those scenes common to a TV movie of the week. One evening right around his second birthday we presented him with a bundle of large, cube-shaped plastic blocks shaped like the letters of the alphabet and another bundle with the numbers 0 through 9. He immediately lined up the ABC's in order and then lined up the numbers. Then he started to double up the numbers, moving the 1 and 0 over to make 10, skipping 11, and moving the 1 and 2 over to make 12 and so on to 21. At first we stared in disbelief, then started cheering him like fans watching a star athlete.

What made the scene different from a TV movie, however, was Walker's reaction to our cheers. A movie would present such a scene as a moment of tragic separation: the mysterious child, locked in a world of his own and more interested in objects than people, suddenly presents a spooky precociousness.

But Walker's main purpose was to impress us. After placing each block in a row, he'd touch it, turn and smile at us for another cheer, every now and then getting up and giving us a hug. Every number was followed by a pause and a proud grin. The scene was thrilling for us, for all of it, from first to last, clearly meant our boy was communicating. We bought him a board with magnetic letters and so he started spelling words ("MICKEY NOUSE" because the set had an extra E but no extra M) and on and on with more words. It became clear that the performance was far more important to him than the spelling. Walker had found a verbal outlet to communicate with his parents because speaking was too hard for him.

He was growing in an unconventional way, we knew, but we weren't terribly concerned, for neither of us had any use for rigid developmental ideas that prescribed alarm as the proper reaction to anything that didn't fit predicted categories of development. We'd read accounts of how Einstein hadn't spoken normally until he was nine, knew that Ellen's own father, a doctor, hadn't spoken at all until he was five, so we felt reasonably sure that a smart boy who loved words was bound to speak well some day.

By the time he was two and a half, however, we wanted some explanation of why he wasn't speaking and wanted to answer a few questions we had: Why was he so smart, yet didn't point at things? Why was he so uninterested in gifts and new toys but so consistently thrilled with people? Why would he only intermittently look at things we pointed to and often avoid our eyes if we were speaking to him? Why was he constantly moving?

Our concerns about him were mixed with not-very-concealed delight: we half-expected a doctor to observe him and say something like, "Well, Mr. and Mrs. Hughes, what you have here is the sort of superior being medical science runs across every, oh, five hundred years or so. Treasure him, keep his spirit alive, and most important, don't get in his way."

So we made an appointment with a very highly-recommended pediatric neurologist, a man friends had referred to as the "Best in the Midwest."

Because I had to teach that morning, Ellen took Walker to the appointment. Moments before the doctor arrived in the examining room, Ellen realized that a completely unforeseen but potentially devastating factor was about to be introduced into the examination: poop. It's difficult to describe the role of poop in our family life, but if we were the UN Security Council, poop, as an issue, would rank with nuclear testing or chemical weapons stockpiling. Walker, still in diapers but a discreet gentleman, always needed to be left alone for this operation. But this was impossible once the doctor entered the room and immediately started looking at his watch. While the doctor looked at him, Walker stood off alone looking intently at a telephone in the room.

As Ellen tried to explain what Walker needed to do, the doctor was already drawing conclusions. "Mom," he said, establishing the status relationships in the room, "Walker seems to be off in a world of his own. He is clearly object-oriented." But Ellen begged him, so he reluctantly let her take Walker into the hall to change his diaper. When they returned, Walker hovered around the doctor with the telephone receiver in his hand trying to hold it up to the face of the neurologist who, unnervingly free of any natural rapport with a friendly child, ignored Walker, openly shrank from his touch, and repeated the statement that Walker was "object-oriented." When Ellen, racing against the doctor's watch, gave him the ultra-abridged version of Walker's devotion to Fred Astaire, his love of words, his affection for people, his intelligence, the doctor had the irritated look of a man who is making a tremendous effort not to roll his eyes.

"So what do you think, doctor?" Ellen nervously asked when he was walking out the door.

"Well, Mom, I want some further tests done, but I don't hold out any hope for this child," was his response.

Just like that: Bang, you're dead, after an examination of ten minutes.

Ellen took a deep breath and put together the kind of sentence I only dream about days after a conversation: "Then I guess that's why God didn't make you his mother."

Getting in the last word, the good doctor shot back: "Down the road, I see the child in an institution." Then he left.

As Ellen related this story to me later that day, I was appalled and amazed. "This is outrageous!" I said over and over as I stormed around the living room. "Walker *Hughes* is object-oriented?!" I shouted, proving it was probably a good thing I hadn't been there for the exam.

When we received his written report, the neurologist neglected to mention his peevish, catastrophic prognosis and, interestingly, didn't use the term "autism" or its parent-soothing substitute, "pervasive developmental disorder." He repeated the description "object-oriented," though, and called Walker "developmentally delayed." He also made an interesting distinction throughout his report. Any observation he made was framed as fact, as in, "Walker displays object orientation." Any observation Ellen made was framed as a somewhat loony opinion with no connection with his general description, as in, "Mother says dances like Fred Astaire" or "Mother says likes bluegrass music." He also recommended a test for giantism—the syndrome of Andre the Giant—in spite of the fact that Ellen had pointed out that

Walker was only in the 90th percentile for height and had tall parents and grandparents.

When we told our friends the story, they too were appalled, amazed, outraged. But not long after this we read the book, *The Magic Feather*, by Bill and Lori Granger, which detailed their near-identical experience with the evaluators of their son, who was labeled retarded despite the fact that he could read beyond his grade level. The Grangers' account of their post-evaluation conversation, in which they decided that the evaluators of their son were full of nonsense, was almost identical with the conversation Ellen and I had.

As time went by and we talked to more and more parents and read other accounts, we realized that our story—far from being the grimly fascinating tale we thought it to be—was actually commonplace and redundant, as predictable as the millionth rerun of an episode of "I Love Lucy" but not nearly so entertaining. If I conjure up a picture of the two of us telling our story at a meeting of parents of children with developmental disabilities, I see our story being greeted with yawns, tell-me-about-it rolling of the eyes, and initiating an escalating competition of horrific accounts, many of them easily far worse than ours.

But that day as Ellen and I sat discussing the disturbing meeting with the neurologist, going over every word he said, we couldn't put the experience in any sort of context. All we knew was that, as wrong-headed as we knew the doctor was, his opinion probably indicated trouble for the future. We knew, too, that though the neurologist had not used the word "autism," that was where his diagnosis was headed. We didn't know much about it, but we'd seen enough films and TV shows to know that a child who behaved oddly, had no speech, looked normal, and was "object-oriented" was probably veering into the category of children who "lived in their own world." But we knew that Walker was, both in a deep and surface sense, living in *our* world, strongly engaged with us and the people in his life.

So our happiness about Walker became mixed with doubt and defensiveness and our glowing reports about his doings to friends and family and doctors would be increasingly met with a mystified reaction that boiled down to: Why are these people smiling?

As we sat on the couch in our living room, speculating worriedly about Walker's future, we noticed him sitting on the floor in the middle of a pile of his books, intently turning the pages of one after another of them, frowning and staring in concentration and interest. Ellen said, "Look at him. He has hopes. He loves words. He loves us. Give up on him? I don't think so!"

We watched as he stared at a picture in a book, stopped, got very excited, then turned the pages back to a similar picture on the cover, stared again, then went back to the picture again, noticing something—a similarity? a difference?—looking like a two-year-old version of an excited astronomer spotting anomalies in star positions in Hubble telescope photographs. We shifted conversational gears and started to chat in our usual movie fan-like, cultist way about how wonderful he was. It hit us that we too were "gifted." We were blessed with a happy, loving, smart little boy who had his whole life ahead of him.

The gift, we knew, would bring with it the job of keeping his hopes and ours alive. But we had no idea, just then, how painfully hard that job would become.

TWO

"Denial"

Of course, we knew there was a name for the territory we were now in. Ellen, the daughter of a doctor, was quite familiar with it, and she even invented nicknames for us, the masters of our new domain: the Duke and Duchess of Denial. Being "in denial," she knew, was the sin of anyone who tried to resist a doctor's negative diagnosis. She would say, "Hey Duke, look at what our young lord is doing." Walker would be listening to a Disney story on tape and turning the pages of the book right on cue.

"Yes, Duchess," I'd say and shake my head sadly. "I hold out no hope for him." Then we'd laugh and admire our little genius.

Despite our belief in his bright future, his silence was the One Horrible Thing that chipped steadily away at that belief. Speech is the biggest developmental issue of all, the *sine qua non*, the quantifiable test of how the child is doing, and Walker was, at three, plainly not doing well. Our first venture into speech therapy was Cheryl, a young, spirited, intelligent woman who loved Walker and whom Walker worshipped. But Cheryl moved downstate and we turned to a speech clinic in a hospital nearby.

I found myself sitting one day with the director of the program looking through a one-way mirror at the speech lesson of Walker and his teacher. I was there because Ellen wanted my opinion on how Walker's speech therapy sessions were going. She was unhappy because the speech therapist had done nothing in the two sessions she'd seen but tell Walker to put various blocks into various holes in a toy mailbox.

So as I watched Walker take directions from the teacher and again do a bang-up job with the mailbox, I pointed out to the friendly director, a gentle-voiced and kindly young woman, that, since Walker could already read and spell over a hundred words, and had clearly mastered mailbox, maybe this constant repetition was not very helpful?

"No, Mr. Hughes. This teaches him cooperation. He must learn to cooperate and follow directions before he learns to read."

"But this is absurd!" I said, my blood beginning to boil. "Walker's probably confused about why he must endlessly do this. It must seem like some kind of punishment to him!"

"Now there, Mr. Hughes," she purred quietly. "We know what we are doing. You should enroll Walker in our day program here at the hospital. You shouldn't try to teach him. That's our job. Your job is just to love him."

The angrier and louder my voice became, the quieter, more patronizing and more musically soothing hers did, and I blew the three weeks of friendly relations Ellen had managed to establish. I was building my reputation as the hot-tempered parent, the one who couldn't be trusted with teachers and therapists. But Ellen agreed with me that this speech clinic was very poor, and we pulled Walker out and took a few months' sabbatical from "Speech" to see what changes might happen through "speech" at home.

IN APRIL OF 1988 Davy was born and our little obsessive baby-worshipping cult became bi-theistic—and very rattled. Our worry about Walker's silence continued unabated while a concern over the new young master filled our heads. Unlike Walker, Davy slept through the night but cried nearly every moment he was awake. As we entered the

searing record heat of the following summer in our air-condition-
ing-free, solar oven of a house, Ellen and I developed new hobbies:
staring at seven-day weather reports in the newspaper, speculating
about when the heat would end, and waiting with anticipation for the
moment each evening when the shadow of the three-flat house across
the street crept up the mini-blinds on our front windows.

I slept in Walker's bedroom, the only room in the house with a
window air conditioner. I was cool, but was awakened each night by
Walker, the fitful sleeper. Ellen and Davy slept on the foldout couch in
the living room in a sort of wind tunnel of three fans. The deafening
roar was punctuated only by the sound of Chicago's elevated rail
trains, locally known as the El, coming from behind the houses across
the street and the occasional war of words over a contested parking
place in front of our house.

Though Davy always slept deeply through the night, I often
wondered what effect all the late-night racket had on his dreams. The
parking spaces on our street—a one-block pocket of two- and three-
flat houses tucked into a dense district of commercial fun—were in
fierce demand. From the front windows of our second-floor living
room, we could hear the dull bass thud of music coming from bars on
Belmont a block away. We could see and hear people—well-off,
sixtyish, dressed-up couples as well as twentysomething punkers
walking by going to restaurants, live theater, and rock music concerts
at theaters like the Vic and Berlin. We could hear strange sounds of
trouble out of range of our windows that we couldn't identify: a fist-
fight? a quarrel? an arrest?

But what was sometimes torture by night was stimulating by day.
Walker's outdoor world was full of people and sights and sounds, and
it seemed to us that any child, autistic or not, could benefit from a
lively world.

THE DUKE AND Duchess, like all parents, did not live in a vacuum.
There were noble friends and relations of all sorts who could also note
Walker's strange silence and speculate about what it meant. My

mother, for one, was in a very difficult position to play the role of caring grandma. Living far away on a ranch in Tennessee, she saw her new grandchild only briefly and so could only wonder and worry about his silence when she was able to see him. On one of her visits, during the blistering summer of 1988, I took Walker and her to our regular hangout, the Dominick's supermarket. This was on the site of the historic Riverview amusement park, which was now a nondescript mall with a Toys "R" Us, a Radio Shack, a Gap, and a staggeringly vast parking lot. Every single last hint of Riverview—the Bobs, the parachute ride, the ferris wheel—had been obliterated except for the trolley tracks that here and there emerged through broken pavement on streets nearby, tracks that once brought thousands to the gritty old carnival that once was.

I hoisted the two-and-a-half-year-old Walker up on my shoulders and hustled them into the supermarket which, unlike our house or car, was an air-conditioned dream. I used to wish I could find some hidden freezer unit there, bring a couple of lounge chairs and a TV, and just camp out. The store was a favorite destination for Walker and me, but also, in an uncomfortable way, a sort of developmental testing center. I had gotten into a bad superparent habit of "teaching" Walker about words and items in the store but really, covertly, testing his knowledge. I sought reassurance from my silent boy that he knew the things he was supposed to at his age.

And so did my mother.

Since her visit was so rare, I was trying to spend some quality time with her and have some quality conversation. So as I pushed Walker in a cart down the cool aisles, I tried out a quality question:

"Mom, this store sits right where the old Riverview used to be. Did you come to Riverview much when you were a teenager?"

I enjoyed hearing her tell about growing up in Chicago, but her attention was all on Walker, who was rocking in the child seat of the shopping cart, smiling, and waving his arms. Picking up an apple, she held it close to his face and went through a process I myself had gone through in this same spot. "What's this, Walker? Do you know what this is?"

Walker looked above the apple, to the side of the apple, anywhere but actually at the apple. His non-reaction jump-started the usual questions in my mind: *Is he hopelessly lost in a world of his own? Is he smart and thus offended by a stupid question? Is he extraordinarily shy and therefore shrinks from random in-your-face vocabulary testing?*

"Is he deaf?" was the question that occurred to my mother.

"No, he's not deaf, Mom. We know he can hear. He can hear a pin drop. Besides, the doctor says his hearing is terrific."

A troubled look came over her face. "I don't know. Maybe he's deaf."

Embarrassed to see my own worry in her eyes, I shuffled us off to finish our shopping.

In the checkout line Walker was starting to lose it; the moment we stopped moving and got into a line or waited for a traffic light his one and a half minute timer activated. He was beginning to cry and kick and squirm, but my mom was herself in a new gear, calmly angling back to the Riverview segment of our conversation.

"You know, I do remember coming to Riverview once."

"Really, Mom?" I said while Walker tried to stand up in the seat of the cart and threw a box of animal crackers on the floor.

"I came here once when I was seventeen or so with Uncle George."

"Really?" I said while pulling out my checkbook with my left hand and lifting Walker out of the cart with my right. The quick-minded cashier, Linda, a veteran of the battles Walker and I have had in her checkout line, acted swiftly, helping bag the groceries and calling over another bagger to help us evacuate.

"The Ozzie Nelson band was playing. Harriet was the singer back then. Remember the 'Ozzie and Harriet' TV show?"

"Sure. Yeah." By now Walker, screaming, was flailing about, tucked under my right arm, and with the other I was navigating the cart to the door. *Only a few seconds and we'll be outside.*

"I felt so grown up to be dancing in the evening," my mother said as we escaped onto the asphalt furnace outside.

In the car on the way home Walker was in the back seat, the hot wind blowing on his red face, as Grandma turned around and offered him a treat. "Here's a cookie, Walker. Like the Cookie Monster says, 'COOKIE!' Can you say 'cookie'?"

Walker didn't take the cookie, didn't look at her. He was grinning and rocking and staring over her head.

She turned to me and said, "Is he deaf? Maybe he's deaf."

OUR WORRY ABOUT him, our suspicion about a coming "autistic" label, was compounded by his strange behavior.

On one of our long walks that same hot summer, I was carrying Walker on my shoulders, and he was jerking up and down and laughing and grinning and helping me discover neck muscles I never knew I had. With one hand tightly gripped around his chubby legs, I tried with the other hand to keep my straw hat on my head and my glasses on my sweaty face.

It was ninety degrees on Belmont Avenue on that Saturday afternoon, but it felt like much more. The concrete, the traffic, and the lack of shade made the heat seem to me like a weather emergency, the summer equivalent of a hurricane or a blizzard. But Walker was having a grand time up there, flirting with the people we passed and looking all around—up at the sky, ahead down the street, into the windows of stores, behind us on the sidewalk—and waving his arms in the air.

I had taken him out to give Ellen and Davy a break. All morning Walker had been either running back and forth through our noisy house (four fans droned day and night) or jumping in place while watching a "Sesame Street" tape. But the shift to outdoors and onto my shoulders hadn't changed the situation much, for he was still jumping in place, only now in a seated position. We were loping down the sidewalk like two street performers when a young, attractive, coolly comfortable-looking woman, microphone in hand, appeared and popped me with a question.

"Excuse me, sir. I'm from NPR and we're doing a story about the weather. Would you mind answering some questions about how you and your son try to beat the heat?"

Little hands were now pushing my hat down over my eyes and a big toddler's body was coming down—thump! thump! thump!—on the back of my neck. I wanted to let out a cackle and say something like "Ha ha! Beat the heat! I tell you I'm mad! Mad I tell you!" But instead I just mumbled "Sorry, can't stop now."

We walked on and a siren blared behind us. I turned around and saw a big hook and ladder truck coming with some difficulty through the dense traffic.

I bent forward, lifted Walker up over my head, and put him down on the curb. "Walker, what a treat! A big fire truck!" I said this speaking directly in his ear (I was still distressingly capable of treating him as though I thought he was hard of hearing) and I held him by the shoulders, crouched down behind him and pointed him at the truck. "Look, here it comes!"

The long, long truck passed slowly just a few feet in front of us, its horn blasting in our ears, but Walker twisted his neck first one way, then the other, and managed—*not to look at it!* This was quite a feat. His sweaty father was behind him and bearing down on him with grim enthusiasm. The truck itself was so vast that it was practically a one-vehicle mini-parade. The same boy who had just now made eye contact with every person on the sidewalk and seemed not to miss a trick wouldn't look at the biggest, most interesting thing on the street.

Frustrated and anxious about him, but curious too, I wondered what was going on. The thoughts came in a familiar set that raced through my mind in a moment. There was this: *It's a joke and he's hassling me. He's seen fire trucks before and it's not such a big deal.* There was this: *Far from being unaware of the truck (because he's autistically "lost in a world of his own") he's actually so excited by the sight that he can't stand it.* And there was this: *The combination of the behemoth truck in front of him and the pressure from the behemoth dad behind him is just too much and he's trying to shut it all out.*

Whatever it was, I thought he seemed a whole lot more *aware* of the truck than he let on.

This last thought fit what I had seen him do in other situations. Sometimes Walker seemed keenly aware of everybody and everything in his world. Other times, especially moments when an adult was eagerly and worriedly pointing something out to him, he seemed to be on a different planet. He might hear his Uncle Pete's name casually mentioned and he would get all excited. But give him a Christmas present, some special, carefully chosen one, and our "object-oriented" boy may show no curiosity about it at all, not even enough to unwrap it. Normal childish greed was no part of his make-up.

Ellen and I had gone around and around about this. We each had had times when we were too tense to think as a new boss or teacher was quickly explaining something complicated and important. Maybe Walker's "black out" threshold—his level of mental and emotional overload—was unbelievably low. Maybe, far from under appreciating the world, he was actually so thrilled by it that he struggled daily to control his excitement.

As I hoisted him back up on my shoulders, I felt lifted by this last explanation. I hadn't had the fire engine bonding event I wanted, but it seemed to me that I had just had, in a quiet subterranean way, something oddly close to it.

WE BECAME ACCUSTOMED to thinking of Walker as our eccentric genius. Unable to make observations and ask or answer questions, he performed communication stunts. We could call out a word to him—"Hey, Walker. Spell 'helicopter'"—and he would stop whatever he was doing, go over to the table and write it for us with his magnetic or block letters, or with chalk on a large blackboard or a crayon on sheets of paper. He would do picture puzzles that were well beyond his age level. He delighted in matching and word association games: He could match words on flashcards that rhyme—words he could not actually say—and do it with great ease.

He was our eccentric artist. Though we could never get him to draw houses, faces, trains, and stick cowboys on stick horses (my own artistic repertoire as a child), he drew inventive rainbows—colors always in the right order—and an elaborate configuration of the sentence "I love you" that looked like poster art. He delighted in sitting

Walker at 4 and Ellen

at the dining room table with us and filling up stacks of computer paper with colorful designs: concentric circles, parallel lines of carefully chosen colors, elaborate flourishy scribbles. He wouldn't center his drawings in the middle of the page; it seemed sometimes as if the drawing was a small piece of a much larger picture that invisibly went off the page.

He was our one-man show. We'd sit in the living room and watch him perform. He'd go to the fireplace, look up at the ceiling in deep thought, and babble sentences. The babble had the rising and falling intonation of real sentences: subjects, verbs, subordinate clauses, little climaxes, parenthetical remarks—but no words. He'd sing snatches of songs we couldn't recognize. He'd use props: Picking up a plastic pal, he'd move him from fireplace to bookshelf to floor and then line him up with other toys. He'd dash to the door, suddenly stop, say something, then skip into the kitchen and say something else. When he was done, the audience—Ellen, I, and now Davy—would cheer and applaud while Walker beamed with pride.

All of this showmanship and communication was directed at us. Never did he go off to another part of the house to play. Never did he tell a story, draw a picture, or do a puzzle simply for his own entertainment. Everything he did seemed to be an attempt to connect with his family.

Though he didn't speak to us normally—he couldn't say, "I feel sick," or "I want that," or, what would have opened up the world for him, nod "Yes" and "No"—we still understood him in a satisfying way. And we fully expected him to start speaking any day, to be, like Einstein, a late talker.

One of the most puzzling things about his silence was that it wasn't total. Unpredictably and rarely, he would utter a sentence. One evening at dinner I casually asked him, "Well, Walker, how's your spaghetti? Is it good? Boy this sure is good." I smacked my lips. "Yum!"

Walker ba-da-binged right back at me: "It's yucky."

Yucky! Ellen and I practically fell backward in our chairs. We were accustomed to carrying on virtual conversations with him in which we supplied question and answer and did all the talking. We'd pause regularly in our chatter, leaving big yawning gaps for him to jump in, but he never did. So this was the jackpot—not just a response but irony! Noel Coward land! Yucky!

Trying to recover and be as casual as possible, we laughed at his joke like it was the most normal thing in the world and tried, like novice jugglers finally getting the hang of the thing, delicately to keep the conversational ball in the air.

"Woa, Walker you sounded just like Oscar the Grouch!" I said, probably radiating expectancy with every syllable. "How's your apple juice?"

No answer, not even a look, not even a smile. He just quietly continued stuffing handfuls of spaghetti into his mouth and getting tomato sauce all over his chubby cheeks.

Ellen offered: "I like the way Oscar always says 'Scram, you guys.' Isn't it funny he lives in a garbage can, Walker?" Again, nothing but enthusiastic spaghetti eating. Conversation over.

WALKER'S INABILITY TO speak cut him off from friends at the very time when he would have started making some. Ellen took him to playgroups and mothers-and-tots programs, but no speech meant no pals.

When I was with him, I often took him to parks and I had a fantasy that some spark of friendship would ignite there.

It was a bright lovely Monday morning in the summer of 1990. Ellen was at home with Davy, and Walker and I were at a park near Lake Michigan. The playground was one of those movie set-like constructions that seemed designed by a sadistic faculty member of the Lincoln Log College of Architecture. Everywhere timber was bolted together creating tunnels and ladders, mazes and hanging bridges. There were towers and slides and parapets and ramparts, all designed to sabotage a tall, bald, and creaky forty-one-year-old man trailing his speedy four-year-old son. More than once I had popped up from some tunnel or pit and slammed my head into a wooden beam, saw stars, and after pulling myself together, had to cast about the forest bed for my eyeglasses.

But the place was paradise to Walker. He always threw himself at it with such enthusiasm and energy, slipped through the labyrinth with such determination and skill, that I didn't mind very much the occasional concussion and humiliation.

Today we'd emerged from Fort Apache into the light and I pulled him over to the swings. Walker couldn't yet actually kick and pump the swing himself, but he loved me to push him. I'd recite Captain Kirk's "Space, the final frontier" speech in his ear as he swung, sometimes with the original words, sometimes with mine:

"These are the voyages of Walker Hughes. His lifelong mission: to say big new words, to seek out new friends and interesting people, to boldly do what no kid has ever done before! Dah, daaah, dah, du-du-du-daaah." Walker loved it and couldn't get enough of it. Neither could I.

That day I was pretty self-conscious about my William Shatner impression, for we were next to a young hip-looking mother pushing her kid in a baby swing. Making small talk with mothers in the park was tough going for me. Too many times I'd made some meek overture only to be met with guarded monosyllabic responses and treated like, well, some bald, spectacled forty-one-year-old Strange Man. So I whispered my speech to Walker, thus assuring that I appeared deeply, authentically strange.

"How old is your boy?" I was surprised to hear her say.

"Oh, he's four."

"He's big for his age." She smiled at Walker and said cheerily to him, "Hi! What's your name?"

After an awkward pause, I said, "Walker." I'd become accustomed to speaking for him, like Mr. Spock doing the "Vulcan mind-meld" on an alien.

"That's a nice name. Where do you go to school, Walker?"

Another pause, and I said, "He has trouble speaking."

"Oh, does he have a speech therapist?"

"He's doing fine, really." Unwilling to get into a discussion of Walker's problems with a stranger right in front of him, right at that moment, as if he weren't there, I looked at my watch and said, "Uh-oh, buddy, it's time for lunch." I smiled at the curious mother and started our getaway, but Walker darted over to the slide where five or six kids were playing.

Without any fanfare, with no triumphant Handel chorus audible in the background, Walker merged with the boys going up and down the slide and fell naturally in line with them—as though to say, "What's your problem, Dad? I do it all the time!" He climbed to the top, locked his legs around the boy in front of him who had his legs wrapped around the boy in front of him, and they all went laughing down the slide to the bottom where they tumbled hysterically into a heap. Then they did it again, and again, and again, while I wondered if I could kidnap these boys for a few weeks and take them home with me.

After ten minutes one of the boys, a freckle-faced red-haired kid, said something to Walker, who smiled but didn't answer. I could see the boy give Walker a "come on, come with us" gesture, but Walker just stood there grinning. Then the friendly gang went off to another area in the playground and left Walker behind.

I could have jumped in with some mind melding and spokesperson work, but I opted to leave the situation alone. I was just too amazed and happy. If this could happen once, I told myself, it could happen some more.

But like his verbal jokes, this moment of play was just another unaccountable blip of success that had the sad side of revealing to us his frustrated desire: he *wanted* to play with friends but didn't know how. Spontaneous games with kids became rarer and rarer.

And our anxiety grew and grew.

THREE

Brothers

One potential friend for Walker lived right under his nose: his brother. We fostered friendship between the boys (foisted friendship upon the boys?) every chance we had.

A turning point happened on a warm Sunday afternoon in April. I was keeping one eye on the Cubs game on TV (remote set on "mute") and the other eye on the pile of student papers I was grading. The front windows were wide open and from time to time the roar of the crowd at Wrigley Field five blocks away wafted into the living room. When the wind was out of the north and no El trains were going by, the occasional brief swelling and receding cheer of the crowd, bringing with it images of ivy-covered walls, happy people, hot dogs and beer, became a sort of airborne Prozac for me.

I looked at the TV to see what had happened but Davy was standing in front of it with a big soft Mickey Mouse ball in his hand. He threw it in the direction of Walker, who was standing at what had become a perpetual station of his at the door. Then a remarkable thing happened: Walker picked up the ball, jumped up on the couch, and *threw the ball back to Davy!* The ball bounced off Davy's chest, so he bent down, picked it up and threw it to Walker. Walker picked it up off the couch and threw it to me. This had never happened before. I had played catch with Walker daily and he had already broken one couch by jumping on it and throwing the ball. But never had the two of them simply *started* playing with each other.

Soon we were all playing.

"This Davy Hughes is just spectacular, isn't he, Harry? Such sparkling form! It's a pleasure just to watch him throw the ball!" I was chattering on and on, trying to mimic the Cubs' announcer Steve Stone. "He's got his hands full today, though. This youngster, Walker Hughes, with a .281 average for every time he bounces on the couch with one sock on and one sock off while facing three opponents, is one hard target to hit."

Ellen was Harry Caray. "Aw, Steve, you said it. All right now. Davy leans back. He throws. It might be. It could be. It is! Walker has it! Holy cow!"

Walker caught the big, soft, Mickey Mouse ball in mid-jump about six inches above the cushions on the right side of the couch, the side he hadn't broken yet. He grinned and clutched the ball tight while coming down, then sprung lightly back up with the ball.

Ellen: "Aw, this is one unpredictable player, folks. Will he throw it to his dad? Will he toss it to his brother? Will he just giggle the rest of the night?" Walker was cracking up with laughter, looking at each of us, teasing us, savoring the moment.

He bounced a few more times and threw the ball to me, and I quickly passed it to Davy who then flipped Mickey to Walker, but Walker was gone. He had just leaped off the couch and dashed down the hall into the corner of the back room from where the rhythmic thud-thud-thud of his feet on the plywood floor reverberated through the house. He was shouting "Ah! Ah! Ah!" and his brother, mother, and father were convulsed with laughter. Davy yelled, "Come back, Walker!" Walker galloped down the hall, bounded into the room and the game resumed, only now Walker was throwing the ball in an upside down position with his head between his legs, backside facing us.

The rules changed from moment to moment, largely at Walker's whim. At three Davy didn't seem clear yet on just how odd his five-year-old brother was, but he must have been as surprised as we were that Walker was playing with him. He hadn't yet had much chance to observe other older boys in action and so thought (or it seemed to us that he thought) that Walker was more normal than he actually was. He knew that Walker could catch and throw better than he could, could print words better, and that he was a big, friendly, strong guy. But he also knew that Walker didn't talk to him and except for this moment, had never initiated play. Big brother was no leader, except of course in moments like this, when, indulged by all of us up to his eyeballs, he was suddenly El Supremo.

This was a very odd form of "catch." But Walker had resisted every other form. At irregular intervals I had taken him outdoors, put a glove on his hand, pitched to him, shown him how to swing a bat. Every single time he looked delighted and excited and tried to cooper-ate—for all of two to five minutes. Then he would be off, racing away as I gathered up the baseball equipment on a run and shouted for him to stop.

But Ellen and I resolutely tried to keep our eyes on what Walker could do, not on what he couldn't. Left to his own devices, he exhib-ited plenty of skill. He threw far and with dead-on accuracy. He had astonishing endurance. He invented new and ever more challenging ways to throw the ball: over his head, with his eyes closed, by spinning it in his fingers and then lobbing it in a high arc, by bouncing it off a wall.

And all of this, always, with a huge smile and a conspiratorial look in his eyes that said, "Wacky, aren't we?" In a No Rules Silly Olympics, Walker would have medaled for sure.

To see him stand on the couch that day, casually flipping the ball around in his hands as he looked at each of us to see who he wanted to tease next, was to glimpse a kid who seemed separated by only the thinnest of barriers from the little athlete and big brother he could be.

BUT WALKER'S DAYS as the more capable and worldly-wise "big" brother were numbered, as we could tell from the dazzling way Davy was growing.

On a morning not long after the baseball game Ellen whispered, "Robert, come here." She was looking over the railing of our bedroom, actually a low wall, which overlooked our living room.

I looked down and saw Walker watching TV in his strenuous aerobic fashion—feet dancing in place about two feet from the screen, arms raised and bent at the elbows, hands waving excitedly back and forth, mouth and eyes wide open. From clear across and above the room we could hear him suck in air as if he were beside himself with shock, as if, say, he'd just seen Big Bird pull a knife on Maria.

Nothing unusual there, I thought.

"No, look at Davy," she said.

Davy was walking rapidly in a circle, clockwise, and talking to himself. I could hear small fragments of what he was saying—pieces like "No, Elmo, give it to Dumbo" and "Tigger, look out!" and "choo, choo, che-che-che-chooo!"—but not enough to tell what he was talking about. He seemed to be doing different voices for different characters: high, low, gruff, sweet, urgent, angry. After one or two complete circuits around the room, he'd skip as though invisibly propelled from behind, say "Boop boop BOOP!" and then continue, re-energized.

I looked at Ellen. "He's telling a story," she said. "I've seen him do this before. He was watching "Sesame Street" but stopped after a few minutes and made up his own story."

"But Tigger's not on 'Sesame Street,'" I pointed out, pedantic cartoon scholar that I was.

"No, he makes up his own stuff. He combines characters and storylines from anywhere, any book, any movie and puts them together in new combinations."

I knew that Davy, at three, had rocketed past Walker in the talking competition. He'd begun speaking at nine months and his rate of word consumption grew geometrically every day. Whenever he heard a new word, he'd not only have to pin down its meaning but spring it on us, sometimes to our complete surprise.

One morning I stepped barefoot on a tiny, sharp Lego astronaut on the floor and the pain sent me hopping across the room and tumbling over a chair. I landed on my shoulder on top of more Lego guys a few feet away.

"Davy, how many times do I have to tell you to pick up your Legos!" I bellowed, slowly enunciating each word.

"You pompous windbag," Davy casually shot back, fast as a Borsht belt comedian.

Later, I asked him where he'd heard the word "pompous."

"Let's see," he said, seeming to scan a large memory bank. "Elephants. In 'Dumbo,' one elephant says it." Long pause. "And in 'Jungle Book,' when the elephants are marching."

So I knew he was doing more than accumulating words—he was tracking them like a lexicographer.

Standing there, staring down at our little storyteller, Ellen and I had the same thought: that Davy was, like Walker, telling stories but also leapfrogging miles past him; not recreating scenarios but making up new ones, starting to put together a populous imaginative world. Did Walker have imaginary worlds of his own? We had no way of knowing.

IN FACT, DAVY was starting to race past Walker in every way, and Walker knew it.

The four of us were sitting at the dining room table on a frigid fall evening. This long, rectangular, beat-up table (we liked to think of it as a fashion choice—Poor Graduate Student Chic) was, like the area around the TV and the kitchen, a major locus for family tragedy and comedy.

We were hovering over the boys, encouraging them and admiring their work as they filled up a stack of computer paper with drawings. Walker made one of his scribbly rainbows with crayons and got big applause from us. Then Davy drew a train, and each car behind the locomotive "carried" a different color of the rainbow. This took our breath away, it was so imaginative and smart.

Then Walker pulled out a single sheet of blank paper and scribbled diagonally across its whole surface with a red crayon. Our euphoria

nose-dived. Here he is, we thought, the big brother completely out-
gunned by the younger.

But he wasn't finished. He put it aside. Then he filled another
blank sheet with orange scribbles and placed it carefully under the first
sheet. Then he took out another sheet, and so on, right through the
spectrum: ROY G. BIV. There it was, "Rainbow in a Stack" next to
"Rainbow on a Train." Without speaking it, we thought: Yes! He's not
only smart, he's jealous! He's openly competing with his brother!
Though he has almost no ability to draw a realistic representation of
an actual *thing*, he has hit upon an intelligent and imaginative way to
up the ante in an impromptu Rainbow Slam!

He tried in other ways to forestall Davy's victory in the child
development race. Early one morning while watching "Thomas the
Tank Engine," Davy suddenly ran up to Ellen, threw his arms around
her, and said, "I love you, Mommy!" Walker, not to be outdone,
escaped his video hypnosis long enough to pull her by the hand over
to his pile of alphabet blocks in front of the fireplace and spell out "I
love you."

This was just an instant; it wasn't followed up by the TV
movie-of-the-week-style breakthrough we every day longed for. I
imagined that some day he'd just explode and rush to spell out the pet
grievances that must have built up in five years of life: "Dad, will you
please stop saying, "How are you, Walker? HOW ARE YOU,
WALK-ER? I'm ticked off that I can't talk, that's how I am! Got it?"

But the "I love you" instant was very precious to us. Ellen and I
would post moments such as this on our mental bulletin boards to
remind ourselves of the normal boy hidden just under the silent
surface. These notes always began "Remember the time Walker . . .?"
When one of us was going into a tailspin of despair about him—fortu-
nately this seldom happened to both of us at the same time—the other
would recite one of these notes.

This always helped—if only a little.

Despite Walker's obvious intelligence and eagerness, Davy, at age
three, was becoming the *de facto* older brother. But he himself did not
seem to know it.

The most successful feat of friendship foisting occurred in the winter of 1990, when Walker had turned five. On that day I learned that I could wrangle both boys over hill and dale *all by myself*. Until I learned to do this, Ellen, Davy, Walker, and I were, outdoors, always a group of four or two groups of two. Walker was presumed to be too wild and too intent on his goals—he *must* go over to that lamppost, he must turn left and not right—that one parent couldn't do both boys outside. I had grown into a habit of taking the two of them to the supermarket by myself, but there I had them physically trapped in two separate carts that I pushed and pulled like a locomotive positioned in the middle of a train.

Out in the open air—that was another matter.

I faced that problem, I thought, brilliantly and courageously. One Saturday in January I took them to the zoo and just demanded they stay together near me—and they actually did! It meant, of course, wild, obsessive vigilance on my part. I had to develop an entirely new range of peripheral vision and new, more agile body movements, especially quicker acceleration from stop to high speed. If the three of us were standing in the crowded and dark Reptile House gazing at a boa constrictor and Walker suddenly skipped off beyond my reach, I could zigzag among the zoo-goers quickly with a careful high-stepping lope while keeping Davy in view with my newly-acquired Vista-Vision. The more I did this, the better I became at it.

My greatest achievement that day was the degree to which I had mastered what Ellen and I termed the "Three F's" of dealing with the boys: "Firm, Friendly, Not Freaked Out." I found that I could achieve this goal outside in public better than at home. Behaving like an idiot who is overwhelmed by his children was all well and good in the house, but in front of strangers in parks and museums and on the sidewalk it was humiliating. So I adopted a better persona. I wasn't Bob Hughes the anxious dad; I was Bill Cosby—funny, happy, maybe a little smug—and way ahead of the kids. This little lie pulled me through many tricky moments and even became a self-fulfilling prophecy on occasion.

Lunchtime that day was very pleasant. Next to the lagoon in the
zoo was a fabulous old Prairie School building called Cafe Brauer. The
three of us marched up the narrow stairs in a wing of the building to an
open-air porch with tables and chairs. It was a warmish winter day in
the fifties and there was no one else there. I unloaded my backpack and
we had a picnic. The space was big and safe, so I let the boys go and let
my guard down. We goofed around, sang, danced, looked down at the
ducks and seagulls and geese in the lagoon and the people passing by,
and just hung out. It was a merry moment of utter normality and I
resolved to have many more.

After that day, on every weekend or holiday, and especially that
summer, I'd pile boys and supplies—audio story tapes, cans of Sprite,
lunches, snacks, changes of clothes, plastic sandbox tools, toy trucks,
battery-powered action figures, and if I was very ambitious,
sleds—into the Escort at about nine a.m. and head out for the parks.
We'd hit only the biggest, most extravagant, wooden-castle,
father's-head-banging parks, sometimes as many as three or four,
meander over to the Lincoln Park Zoo for lunch, and end the day at
the North Avenue beach.

We'd leave Ellen in her bathrobe tapping away at the Macintosh
and return in the afternoon to find her still in her bathrobe, fingers
flying over the keyboard, eyes glued to the screen. She knocked off
press releases, annual reports, medical brochures, and children's encyclopedia chapters during our junkets. Writing with the boys in the
house was next to unthinkable: Walker presented too many
minute-by-minute challenges. So Ellen learned to work at the
break-neck speed of a "Front Page" reporter and wring every free
minute for what it was worth.

It was my finest hour. I loved being out with them, seeing them
play together (or at least "parallel play" together) as they dashed
through tunnels and stomped over bridges; hearing them giggle as I
pushed them on swings next to each other and recited the introduction to the old "Superman" TV show; seeing them smile as they ate
their sandwiches at Café Brauer with their Cubs caps tilted back on
their heads, their eyes shining.

CHILDREN, ELLEN AND I knew, accept whatever their family situation is, however bizarre or even outrageous, as normal—up to a point. Davy was still going along happily enough thinking that Walker was OK. He followed our lead in treating Walker as a fun, if very different, kid. But with school on the horizon, a revealing test of sorts was about to be given. Would Walker go to school, acclimate himself, and take the lead in stepping out into the world?

When I was Davy's age, I desperately wanted to be as old as my sister Pat, who was in second grade before I was old enough to go to kindergarten. I screamed and fought to get on the bus with her, and my parents had to install a deadbolt at the top of the door to keep me in the house when her bus arrived each morning. It was very hard to imagine such a scenario happening in our own house unless Walker greatly stepped up his ability to socialize.

A day of reckoning was coming. We braced ourselves for Walker's first introduction to school where, we thought, he'd seem even in the kindliest light to be like a visitor from space.

FOUR

Yes and No

The summer before Walker attended pre-school Ellen and I became truly alarmed about his silence. How could he get through a single day of school with so little ability to speak?

So I created a project for myself. I would teach him to reply "yes" and "no" to questions. A person who could master "yes" and "no," I reasoned, could have the world at his feet. He wouldn't even have to say the words—he could nod, tap his foot, rub his tummy, pat his head, stick out his tongue.

My methodology was to find things I knew he wanted or didn't want and trick him into answering.

So I became a monster of questioning. I'd shoot questions at him like a panicky machine gunner. *Rat-tat-tat* I'd go: "Do you want some spaghetti, Walker?" "Do you want some ice cream?" "Would you like to go to the park?" "That Bugs Bunny! Isn't he funny, Walker?" "Are you tired?" "Do you have a headache?" "Are you feeling good?"

On and on I went. We knew about many of his preferences because he'd eat or not eat, play with or not play with things presented to him. But the closest he'd get to the verbal reply I wanted was repetition. I could say, "Would you like some Eggo Mini's?" And he might, but not reliably, repeat "Mini's." This, of course, was a form of "yes."

But not to him. In his mind there seemed to be a critical difference, for he would not under any conditions say the magic words "yes" or "no." To do so was to cross some boundary into the land of speech that he would not or could not cross.

We were driving past Blockbuster Video, a store that was becoming like Mecca to him. "Hey, Walker. Do you want to get a video?"

"Video!" he responded. His eyes brightened and he looked into my face.

"Do you want to get a sing-along tape?"

"Tape!"

I pulled into a parking space, turned off the ignition and said, "OK, man. Do you want a tape?" Then in a mock-conspiratorial whisper: "Now say 'yes' or 'no.'"

"Yes or no."

"Walker, we won't get out of the car unless you say 'yes,'" I paused a few beats, "or 'no.'"

"No."

"Do you want a tape?"

"Tape."

We were Abbott and Costello, but only to a nonexistent outside observer. For me it was agony. As my anger rose, I'd have to remind myself to stop, pull myself together, and switch gears. No matter how clever or stupid, no matter how patient or upset I was, he always escaped.

His speech problem in general was not what I was accustomed to thinking of as a "speech" problem at all. He could enunciate anything, though he often—seemingly intentionally—slurred syllables or sounds. He would also make up his own pet words and phrases that were close but slightly off for the thing he wanted. When he was younger and he wanted his Nuk brand pacifier, he'd say "Nuk please nuk-off!" He would add a final 't' sound to almost any word—"bedt," "juicet," 'Davyt." (That 't' seemed like a kind of exclamation point to us.) Whenever I came home from school, he would shout "Hey, deedee!", a phrase which, strangely and embarrassingly enough, took us a long time to realize meant "Hi, Daddy."

I thought *Well, he can spell. That should help at school. He can touch letters of the alphabet and spell out words. Maybe I could make two signs saying "yes" and "no" and he could point to one or the other.*

But he never pointed at anything. Ever.

This, even more than his avoidance of yes/no, seemed the starkest sign of his separation from the social world. Pointing, he seemed to sense, meant, "OK, here I am, a player in the game."

His evasion of the game took more effort and ingenuity than simple capitulation would have. His avoidance was all of a piece: it couldn't be catch, it had to be bouncing-on-the-couch-and-running-down-the-hall catch; "house" and "park" had to be "house*?*" "park*?*"; "spaghetti with cheese" had to be "spaghetti *something else*"; "That's an elephant" became a grand production: the letters "e-l-e-p-h-a-n-t" pronounced loud and clear and followed by lining up the the magnetic letters on a board.

COMPOUNDING OUR WORRY about his fate in school was the fact that, by age five, he had already more or less "flunked sandbox" several times. Ellen had taken him to various North Side Moms-and-tots-type groups where his inability to speak and play like other children made them both outcasts. These playgroups were Ellen's first experiences on the front line, the edge where Walker and society met. Ellen was the combat officer; I was the benign coward who only stood and waited. While I taught class or graded papers in peace and safety, she was out witnessing Walker's failures to connect and taking it on the chin from mothers who didn't really want their children near this strange boy.

But we were determined to get him, belatedly, into pre-school. His excitement when he was near other kids, combined with his intelligence and energy and happy nature, made us—very guardedly—hopeful.

We found a good church school only two blocks from our house, and on a sunny day at noon in the early fall Ellen strolled there with Walker. I hid out with Davy, watching "Dumbo," pacing back and forth across the living room, and waiting for the report.

When I heard their footsteps on the front stairs and heard Ellen say through the open front window, "Slow *down*, honey," in a wearied tone, I knew right away that all had not gone well.

Walker raced in and sat down on the floor with a book. Ellen looked at me, sat down on the couch, and stared at nothing

"Not good?" I asked.

"You know how they say the most painful thing you can go through is to be a patient in the burn unit of a hospital?"

I thought, *Uh, oh, a metaphor. This must be really bad.*

"Well, that's what it was like. Like getting my skin peeled off."

This was the first time Ellen had used this comparison, and from then on we had a new term to sum up any humiliating public scene with Walker.

The first "skin-off experience" went this way:

When they got to the door of the school building, Pam, Walker's teacher, cheerily whisked him into the classroom, and Ellen went upstairs to sit around a table with the other mothers for coffee and camaraderie and a pleasant introduction to the school by the principal.

Ellen had sat there for less than five minutes before Pam, flustered-looking, came to the door and pointed to Ellen and gave her a toothy, sheepish-looking grin, the international sign for "Come here; there's trouble." Ellen didn't know it at the time, but those five minutes turned out to be the length of her membership in the Club of the Mothers of Normal School Children.

Walker had skipped into the room and made a beeline for a large water toy: plastic buckets and gears and aqueducts channeling water up to platforms and waterfalls and paddlewheels. To other kids, this toy was a great chance to turn gears and paddlewheels; to Walker it meant one thing—a chance to splash water everywhere, on kids, on teacher, and above all, on himself. If Walker had uttered some kind of wild little kid patter while splashing everybody—"Wow! Look at me, everybody!"—it wouldn't have seemed so strange. But he did it silently, with a big, sweet, smile on his face, and he must have seemed a little too weird. With all the kids and the two other teachers staring at Ellen, Pam said, "We wonder if you could stay in the classroom with Walker for the first few days until he gets used to it?"

"Oh, sure," Ellen said pleasantly while she changed Walker's shirt. (Clean, dry clothes never lasted long on Walker, and Ellen had a habit of taking spare shorts and shirts with her.) She spent the next few hours sitting with him when he sat in a circle, sitting with him at a table to do finger paints, holding hands with him when the children stood and sang in a circle. Whenever she stepped back to give him some freedom, he always fell back too.

He was delighted to be there—too delighted. No matter what the task, he usually became so excited that he eventually started lunging at her, biting her, yelling, throwing things and jumping in place. Then Ellen had to take him into a corner or out of the room until he calmed down.

The "few days" grew into a few weeks. I took my turn shadowing Walker at school, but he did even worse with me than with Ellen. Everything about me was ill-suited for this work. First, I was a man, the only man in the room and a great oddity to the children—Walker's pet bear, a distraction to everybody. Second, I was bad at it. A teacher myself, I'd get impatient with keeping my mouth shut when I thought a teacher should do one thing instead of another. Third, I had only two physiognomic gears: smiling and frowning, and I simply couldn't smile that long.

So Ellen was the designated parent for the front-line duty of grinning and trying to appear in control of our out-of-control little boy. She discovered the sensation of having her parenting skills under perpetual review by three teachers and twenty confused pre-schoolers, and answering sweet-voiced little questions:

"Why are you here?"

"Why won't Walker talk?"

"Why does he jump up and down all the time?"

"Why does he eat the clay?"

"Why does he spill the paint?"

Understanding and helpful as the teachers were, Ellen knew that they couldn't really enjoy having a parent there observing them. So she tried to be there but simultaneously not be there; be a sort of all-around teacher's aid as well as Walker's personal valet. She knew, and she knew the teachers knew, that the normal route for a boy with big developmental trouble was early labeling and public school special education. This booster-mom-in-the-classroom stuff was very unconventional, especially since Walker often seemed like such a hopeless case. So on top of every other emotion she was experiencing, Ellen felt like a sort of poster girl for Parental Denial.

In every way, her job was a stomach-twister, and there was no end in sight.

Still, as the first year wore on, the three teachers—Pam, Meg, Amy—never showed any signs of giving up. As long as Ellen was willing to keep trying, as long as she could maintain her hopes in the face of Walker's tantrums, his biting, his yelling, his flamboyant bizarreness, so were they. This was a tribute to the dedication of the teachers, but also to Ellen's talent for dealing with people. Where I tended to assume combat mode with people, Ellen acted on a mantra of hers, one that she had learned from her mother and that came straight from the heart: "People will be just as good as you expect them to be, and no better." She approached therapists, teachers, and doctors as though each one was a sort of Robin Williams-style big-hearted miracle worker. "Why, you wonderful person," she seemed to say, "I know you'd do anything to help my boy." Amazingly, they often did.

This approach got better results than my attitude that somehow communicated the message, "Look, you toad. Help my son, dammit!"

In fact, an unspoken protocol developed between us: I had free reign to make judgements and take action on the domestic front, but foreign policy was the province of Ellen. When I went to meetings with Ellen, my job was to look like I *could* say something powerful and insightful if I really wanted to but was ominously waiting for the right moment.

IN ADDITION TO the teachers, Walker's classmates were another surprise. We had heard that young children could be especially cruel to kids who behaved as strangely as Walker did. But this was far from being the case. Unlike most adults, the kids picked up on the fact that Walker enjoyed school and wanted to communicate, that there was a normal boy to be seen through the chaos of all his batty behavior.

They liked him.

When the class sang "Happy Birthday" to Walker, he rushed from Ellen's side to the front of the classroom, faced everybody with a big smile and a red face, and firmly planted his fingers in his ears. After the song, the children all cheered, and one of the girls said to Ellen, "Yay! He's got his fingers in his ears! That means he really likes this!"

When the children performed a song about the growth of a flower by forming a circle, curling up into a ball and then slowly unfolding to a full standing position with arms uplifted Busby Berkeley-style, Walker was the only one who remained frozen in the fetal-crouch. As Ellen's heart sank, one boy shouted, "Walker is just a seed now, but he'll grow later and he'll be the biggest flower of all!"

Being the parent on the firing line was very rough, but it had its own glimmering rewards.

When the school year ended and we tried to take stock of how Walker had done, we had to admit that he hadn't made much progress. He wasn't playing with children any better; he wasn't sitting still; he wasn't following directions. He loved school and marched off for it with zest every morning, but he was like a fanatical, inept baseball fan who miraculously finds himself in spring training with the pros.

And, to my grinding chagrin, he was no closer to "yes" and "no."

But soon something happened that made all this roiling child development concern seem very unimportant.

WHEN WALKER RAN down the hill away from the statue of General Grant and showed no signs of stopping, I knew there was something wrong. It was a steamy hot sunny day in August, the sort of summer day in Chicago when the humidity seems like a visible vapor clinging to trees and grass, and I was on the Lincoln Park leg of one of my six-hour expeditions with the boys.

They normally did a good job of tramping in the direction I chose, but this day Walker suddenly took off and ran down the slope away from the monument toward the lagoon.

I yelled, "Walker, you get back here now!" and waited and watched until I determined that he was approaching the point from which I couldn't catch up to him. Would he run into the water? I had no idea, but I wasn't about to find out. I grabbed Davy by the shoulders and said, "Stay right here. Don't move."

I took off running and shouting, "Stop!" but he continued racing away from me. Overtaking him a few yards before he reached the edge of the water, I started snarling and growling threats in his ear and yanking him by the arm. "You must *never* run away like that. You *have* to stay with me. Now Davy is way up there alone!" I pulled Walker's hand, but he wouldn't come. He started screaming and trying to bite me, alternately jumping up at me and pulling away. There were dozens of people all around us. I snarled at them too.

I picked him up, tucked him under one arm, pushed his head away from me with the other arm, and bounded back up the hill to where Davy was dutifully waiting and perhaps slipping the whole scene into a growing file labeled, "My Dysfunctional Family."

I was upset. This had never happened before—at least to this degree—in a whole summer of happy expeditions.

As I stalked along with the boys past General Grant on his noble steed that day, I was rattled and worried about Walker, my confidence badly shaken.

After hauling the screaming Walker up the hill, I sat him in the grass and asked him, "How do you feel? Does your head hurt?" I tapped first my head, then his. "Does your throat hurt?" I rubbed by fingers on his throat. "How about your stomach? Do you want a drink? Try to tell me, Walker." This time, for once, I didn't push "yes" and "no."

Walker just looked away silently, not his usual reaction, which was more engaged with the issue if not satisfying to me.

"He can't talk, Dad," Davy reminded me.

"Right," I said, irritated and worried. "Let's get over to the lake and get into the water." I said this as happily as I could, trying to get back to my better self. "We'll cool off."

By the time we were crossing the arch of the big footbridge over Lake Shore Drive, I had put the mystery of Walker's outburst out of my mind. This bridge was a major attraction on our trip, and we stood there a few minutes looking down at the six lanes of cars and buses roaring beneath our feet, at the crowds swarming past us, at the lake and beach stretched out in front of us. There was an exciting, fake-danger, amusement park-ride feel to standing there, safe but still close to the speeding cars. We all three were smiling and back to our usual enthusiastic summer expedition mode.

But not for long. Once we were unloaded and in beach sprawl format, Walker rocketed away again, this time straight down the shore where I could easily lose him in the crowd. "Stay here!" I yelled at Davy, and took off after him. Capturing him about a hundred feet away, I grabbed him by the shoulders and spoke loudly and slowly over the din of waves, wind, and crowd: "Ne-ver-run-a-way-from-me! *Never!*" But Walker was looking off at the lake; not a flicker of emotion registering on his face.

I shifted my hands to either side of his head and forced him to look at me. I stared into his face and mentally raced through a desperate litany of questions: Was he confused by the words "never run away"? Was he too excited to calm down enough to understand the words? Was he angry at me for something and trying to get back at me? Was he feeling sick—a headache or stomachache or earache—and desperate about his inability to talk about it? Was he purposely behaving in a way he knew would force me to take him home?

Was he? Was he? Was he?—the questions familiar from late evening discussions with Ellen were hellishly urgent to me right now. Ellen wasn't here, Walker was blowing up and the car was far away, parked in the zoo lot under the watchful eyes of General Grant.

Twice more Walker tore away from our spot. On his last getaway, after a long chase, it was my turn to explode. I yelled at him, spanked him (spanking, for the record, never, *ever* worked), and told Davy we had to go. This was the signal for Davy (quite understandably) to lose it, and so I staggered back to the car across a long stretch of burning sand, past an audience of staring sun-worshippers and frisbee-throwers, laden with beach equipment and screaming boys.

It was not my finest hour.

Driving home, I felt guilty about putting the boys through what turned out to be a kind of Bataan Death March and resolved to read the signs of coming disaster more intelligently.

BUT THE NEXT morning at 6:15 disaster already seemed to be upon us.

Walker had been awake for half an hour, vomiting and staring fixedly off at the walls. We'd pulled out the sofa bed and Ellen put him down next to her. As he lay there, he became more and more rigid, tapping his finger on his pillow and staring. I couldn't stand it any longer. "I'm taking him to the emergency room right now," I said as I pulled on some clothes.

Just before I picked him up, we couldn't detect any breathing and his body was bent at the waist and stiff as though frozen. I tucked him under my arm and ran down the back steps to the car. The hospital wasn't far away, but since Walker wasn't breathing it seemed like many miles between the house and help.

I sped through the streets, cutting through red lights like a TV detective, and talked to him nonstop, gibberish like "You're gonna be OK" alternating with "Talk to me, dammit!"

I carried him, bent and rigid as a board with his eyes wide open, into the emergency room. The doctors and nurses moved swiftly. When describing his condition I found myself using the word "autistic-like," though I had never used it before. It was my shorthand way of describing him, for it was important for them to understand that when healthy he didn't speak, so that they wouldn't misinterpret his silence when he gained consciousness. If he gained consciousness.

Their first move was to get me out of the way. I was led to a small room with a chair and a phone where I waited and concentrated, with all my might, on breathing. After about ten minutes a doctor came in and said that Walker had had an epileptic seizure, that he hadn't been breathing when he arrived at the hospital, and that they hadn't been able to revive him yet. "But he'll live, right?" I asked.

"We just don't know yet," he said.

Shortly after the doctor left, a social worker arrived to talk to me and make sure, I suppose, that I didn't pass out or flip out. She was kindly and sensitive, but to me she was like an angel of death who had appeared only because they did not expect Walker to pull through.

THREE HOURS LATER Ellen and I were standing next to Walker's bed. He was alive and breathing but still unconscious. We were relieved in the way near-death experiences have a way of making one appreciate life, mere life, but we were still terribly anxious. He hadn't shown any awareness of his surroundings since his seizure had begun early that morning. They had explained that seizure disorders were common among autistic children, and that a serious seizure such as Walker had could very well mean brain damage.

As we hovered over him, he suddenly opened his eyes, sat up, looked around the room, and said, "Doctors."

"Oh, Walker, hello, man!" I said, amazed and laughing, and put an arm around him.

"Yes, honey, *doctors*," Ellen said, stroking his curly hair. "You went through a lot, but you're OK now. You're in the hospital."

He tried to look around us, past us, over us, and said quietly, "No doctors today."

"What was that honey?" Ellen asked.

Walker stared into her eyes and said it again, louder, the sweetest thing we'd ever heard him say, "No doctors today."

Ellen and I looked at each other wide-eyed and giddy with relief. *His mind is just fine*, we both thought at the same time, *and we're having a conversation!*

And I finally, finally, had my "no."

FIVE

Child Development to the Rescue

"No doctors today" fast developed into other beautiful negations: "no movie today," "no peanut butter today," "no bath today," and my favorite, the global "no *this* today." His "yes" took the form of repetition, as in: "Walker, do you want to go to Uncle Pete's house?"

Affirmative answer: "Uncle Pete!"

Negative answer: "No Uncle Pete today!"

It was a clear advance in speech, but it didn't balloon into my yes/no fantasy: he and I capturing the world and naming it with questions and answers. He wouldn't consistently answer me, even when I knew some strong desire—like going to a park—was at stake. And, maddeningly enough, his "no *x* today" sometimes had nothing to do with "no," but was more a way to get a Walker-style conversation going.

One fall evening in 1991 we were watching the final forty-five seconds of a Bulls game on TV, and the Bulls were behind by four, so we were glued to the set expecting Michael Jordan to win the game momentarily. Walker, who was behind us in his corner of the dining room eating toast, yelled out, "NO SPAGHETTI TODAY!"

I got up, one eye still on the game, and said, "You don't have spaghetti. You have toast. Finish it and then you can have something else."

"NO SPAGHETTI TODAY!" This time he shouted the words two inches from my face.

"What are you saying?" I asked, my game eye now fixed on him and the temper lobe of my brain beginning to throb. "Do you want spaghetti?"

"Spaghetti!"

"But you have to finish your toast first."

"NO SPAGHETTI TODAY!"

Game over. Bulls win.

ANOTHER RESULT OF the seizure was that it ushered us into a new world of medications. The neurologist at the hospital prescribed Tegretol, a drug she said would help control his seizures but also work to control his outbursts. We had resisted behavior-modifying drugs with all our might up until then. We preferred helping him learn to control himself in the context of daily living; only this, we thought, would give him confidence in himself and a firm foundation as he got older. But there was no choice: Tegretol could mean the difference between life and death.

We didn't know it at the time, but we were on our way to becoming the celebrity customers of our local Walgreens pharmacy. At our peak, even part-time clerks recognized us approaching far away down the aisle and called up our records before we reached the counter.

We vowed not to let a night-time seizure take us by surprise again. So for the next year Walker slept with Ellen on the fold-out couch in the living room and I slept upstairs in the mezzanine. Despite this precaution he seized twice more in the night, necessitating two more French Connection-style drives through city traffic.

WALKER'S TROUBLES WERE multiplying in a classic mar-
riage-smashing way: every thought, every move we made became
affected, often determined, by his disability. A child psychiatrist told a
couple we knew that 90 percent of parents of autistic children eventually divorce.

But here was our nice surprise, in a way the luckiest single fact of
the Walker saga: Ellen and I looked at our boy the same way. We
enjoyed him and admired him. We liked to study him, speculate about
him, discover his strengths. We thought his pluses were more interesting and important than his minuses. This got us through the day, for
every moment seemed to involve some possibility of legitimate dis-
agreement—methods of discipline to stop a tantrum, strategies to
encourage speech, which experts to consult and whether to consult
experts at all, the kind of schooling he should have.

Walker, and later Davy, became our reason for being, our marital
Manhattan Project. We considered our disagreements to be like those
of scientists doing an experiment together who are equally excited
about their work.

"I'M JUST NOT ready to hand him over to the Developmental Police,"
I was saying to Ellen late on a November night. Walker was tempo-
rarily asleep in his bedroom, to be moved soon onto the living room
sofabed. "I don't think they know what they're doing." I had put "Late
Night with David Letterman" on mute five minutes earlier, so alarmed
was I about her suggestion that we try to get some advice from experts
about Walker. My memory of the neurologist who "holds out no hope
for this child" still burned.

"Just listen," she said. "I don't want anything to do with therapists
either. But I think we ought to see if they have any tricks we can use.
Walker's doing better but he's not where he should be to handle
school. He's not doing well at the pre-school and we can't approach
first grade the way we did pre-school anyway."

Our united front regarding What To Do About Walker was deep
and real, but there were differences. I was the distrustful reactionary,

Ellen the trusting liberal; I was the family philosopher who tended to argue with people; Ellen was the diplomat-negotiator and PR person to the outside world.

"But just the other day I had such a good reading and talking session with him," I said. "In some ways he's doing better and shows promise."

"I know, I know, it's true. But sessions like that seem to be getting rarer and rarer and in school he has to do OK every day. A teacher can't give him the kind of attention we do."

"Don't you think the experts will see only his shortcomings and just nail a label on his forehead?"

"Yes, yes, that could be. It probably *will* be. But we have to give it a try. I don't know, maybe we can build connections through them to tutors and teaching methods that will help."

I turned around on the couch and looked out the window. It was nearly midnight. Our little street was, as usual, bright with the blinking rear red lights of gridlocked SUVs, double-parked and hungry for parking spaces.

"OK," I said. "Let's find some people to talk to," which meant, *Please, please, please, Ellen, you* find some people to talk to. You've got the social skills in the family; I'm just the humble thinker.

I knew that Ellen was right. The remarkable session I'd had with Walker two days earlier was just that—remarkable for its rarity.

It had been a cold weekday afternoon. Walker was wearing purple sweatpants and a black turtleneck with a red sweatshirt over it. With his gold curls and pink cheeks and big grin he looked like an advertiser's dream of a gorgeous, trouble-free kid. Walker and I were humming along. "Go ahead, Walker. You're doing great!"

Walker looked down at the large sheet of paper where I'd written a sentence in magic marker. I hunched near his head to hear him. He was whispering, but whispering very clearly, every word I'd written: "I—love—to—go—to—Grandma—Ruth's—and—Grandpa—Jack's—house—It's—wonderful—to—see—the—horses—and—cows."

"That's fantastic, man!" I told him as he grinned into my face, picked up the oversized sheet of paper, and ran up and down the hall with it.

He was skipping all over the house with glee and only returned when I said, "Hey, Walker. Come read this one."

He ran back to the table, stopped, took a deep breath, and looked down at the words like a child viewing a fireworks display for the first time

Why did he love reading these sentences so much? Certainly, it was a way for a non-speaker to communicate. We worked hard to write sentences that reflected what we thought were his opinions, his likes and dislikes. So when he read them he was giving voice to something he'd never enunciated before. And just as certainly, he was getting praise from us for a real accomplishment: he was justly proud of himself.

Less certainly, but in the range of plausibility, was that the words were like friends. For a long time, after first starting to watch "Sesame Street," he went to bed with a block shaped like the number 6. Sometimes he went to sleep with the word MICKEY MOUSE spelled out in block letters on the edge of his bed. Two years earlier he was running around the house holding sheets of paper with favorite "Sesame Street" terms printed on them like "One Way" and " Exit" and "School Bus."

He got down to business and read my next sentence: "It's—ter—ri—fic—to—take—long—trips—in—the—car. I—like—to—look—out—the—window—at—the—farms." Though he'd probably never seen the word "terrific" before, he came fairly close to sounding it out phonetically.

"Utterly incredible, man!" I said and gave him a kiss. He took the sheet of paper away for another victory lap.

This routine permitted me actually to hear what his voice sounded like (high and sweet) and I got the illusion that he was telling me something. But the routine didn't always work. At moments of great agitation, when it seemed to us that he must certainly have something to say but couldn't form the words, presenting him with a piece of

Walker at 4

paper with sentences written on it and asking him to read could be a huge mistake.

I got up, walked over to the front windows and laughed. Walker's happiness was amazing and unaccountable to me. Across the street was an empty lot between two very tall three-flat houses, and through the lot I could see the rush hour El trains thunder into and out of the Belmont station a half block away. Ellen and I had come to think of the El as a sort of colorful big loud neighbor. For Walker the train was a source of endless, vigilant fascination. He could hear it coming long before we did, run to the window, and wait for it to appear between the buildings.

It struck me how vastly different Walker's childhood was from my own. When I was six years old in the mid-1950s and looked out my front window at 5 p.m., what I saw was a green, sleepy, Levittown-style Chicago suburb. Unlike Walker, I couldn't read at all. My first introduction to reading was at age seven in the first grade and my first stories were about the relentlessly dull adventures of David and Ann, the Catholic school equivalent of Dick and Jane. I did not run up and down the halls of my house in ecstasy clutching David and Ann to my chest. I did not love words and cling to them as pals.

Unlike Walker, I had a best friend, Bruce Miller, and all I had to do to see him was tell my parents where I was going and go. It seems preposterous now, but I would walk alone out the unlocked front door, walk alone down the side of the street (there were no sidewalks), and stroll into a fun, bustling house very much like my own.

But my own son was like a prisoner. We had three locks on the front door, two to keep bad characters out, one—a small sliding bolt placed at the top of the door—to keep him in. He got out every day with his friendly, affectionate prison guards, his parents, and his house was filled with entertaining gadgets and gizmos, but he was trapped nonetheless.

Walker had no Bruce Miller, no freedom to explore his world, no tight little community of friends, but judging by our little reading session, he had moments of great fun when he was very proud and happy.

Even during a sunny moment like this, however, I felt the cloud of anxiety ready to roll in over my head when the euphoria had passed. Walker at some point would refuse to continue with the "lesson" and return to some repetitive action like jumping in place or staring at a point of light or running back and forth on a route through the house.

As Ellen said, he *was* frighteningly far from sitting still and listening to a teacher.

WE BOTH KNEW what the likeliest label for Walker was. The lack of speech, the staring at reflected light, the arm-waving, the seeming inability to play with toys or other children in a normal way, the inexplicable excitement, the maddening jumping in place—all of it would be seen by an expert as mainline autistic.

"Is Walker autistic?" our joke (spoken only to each other) would go. "Is the Pope Catholic?"

But from what we'd read and heard, the word "autistic" seemed like the grossest slander applied to our boy. The word created the visual image of a child who is off in a corner, rocking back and forth, lost in a world of his own, so fiercely inner-directed that he can't form bonds with the people in his life. We believed that if professional child developers no longer saw him as the product of a refrigerator mother, they nevertheless saw him as a refrigerator *boy*.

We feared that if the word got pasted onto Walker—who was smart and happy, who loved to be with people and had formed strong bonds with his parents, who was certainly growing and doing better in certain respects—the word itself would shut down curiosity about him in relatives, teachers, possible friends—even us; that his most desperate attempts at communication would be dismissed as "more inappropriate stuff from that autistic kid."

We feared that if Walker was treated as a boy afflicted with an intractable, unbending condition—a permafrost of the mind—he might freeze up and become the rigid boy everybody told him he was.

We'd seen a prominent child psychiatrist on TV, one noted for his sensitivity and his belief in the individuality of each child and his grasp of the latest research—and we weren't impressed. He said that autistic children have no natural inclination to hug, smile, or say "Thank you," but with the right training, they can be taught in a limited way to do such things. A hug from an autistic kid, he said, doesn't mean what parents think it means, for "they do it by rote" to "get something from you."

He implied strongly—this wise, cutting-edge expert who was attempting to dispel common myths about autism—that autistic children have no normal feelings but with the right training and early intervention can be taught to *mimic* normal feelings.

My God, we thought. Does he mean that when Walker, unbidden, put his arms around Ellen on her birthday and said, "I love you," we misunderstood the gesture? That, unlike a normal child, he was trying to "get something" from his mother? That he's a sort of Martian child who bears a superficial resemblance to an Earthling but who down deep is from a race apart?

And does he mean that there is some easy, universally agreed-upon distinction between showing love to "get something" and showing love to "give something"?

We wondered, *If a top-of-the-line psychiatrist is in fact so stupid, what about the ordinary ones?*

From this expert's point of view, our whole daily project of staring at Walker and trying to piece together the puzzle of *why* he did what he did was a fool's enterprise powered by denial.

WE WERE DISCOVERING that the tendency to think that there are two kinds of people in the world—the "normals" with "real" feelings and the other kind who have crossed over into the Land of the Labeled—wasn't limited to experts and therapists. With some friends, too, Ellen and I seemed like the James Stewart character in the movie "Harvey" who chatters on and on about his wise, quotable but invisible six-foot tall rabbit pal.

(SCENE: AN OLD friend, one who knew us before children as a sane couple, is over for a rare dinner. The friend is distracted from her plate of lasagna by Walker, who is ten feet away watching a Muppet tape this way: He stands off to the side of the TV set, his fingers in his ears and his elbow touching the set. He very slowly creeps up to where he can peek sideways at the screen a little, then comes forward a little more, then a little more, and then, looking surprised and breathless, quickly steps back again.)

FRIEND: Uh, what's Walker doing?

ME *(excited to be on my favorite topic)*: I think he's trying to see the characters from the side. He can't believe they're not in three dimensions and so he keeps trying to catch them the way they're supposed to be.

ELLEN: Don't you think he's trying to sneak up on the Muppets, join in the fun, and somehow jump into the screen?

ME: Yeah, that seems possible too.

FRIEND *(squinting slightly)*: Really?

ELLEN: You know how actors enter and exit a stage from the side. He might be doing the same thing. Maybe he's surprised not to see himself on the screen.

FRIEND *(puzzled and staring at Walker)*: Wow.

ME: Yeah, remember the night he shouted: "I'm in the movie! I'm in the movie!"

ELLEN: Since Walker doesn't have friends, we think he might see the Muppets as reasonable substitutes.

FRIEND *(nodding head, trying to be polite)*: Yes. So, Bob, how are your classes going?

I was always of two minds about such scenes. One side of me was angry about the friend's refusal to take us seriously: the no-response response, the noncommittal shake of the head assenting to nothing in particular, the sad agreement with whatever. Ellen and I were like alcoholic friends who couldn't be spoken to about their drinking problem in mid-martini.

Another side of me—and this was even more infuriating—understood the friend completely. How would I react if I were in the friend's position? Before Walker, I never would have had any patience with this Amateur Analysis of the Child by the Proud Parents. Even more than most people—being academic and extra-literal-minded—I was committed to the normal/abnormal dichotomy: the normals were free to move about the cabin; the abnormals needed to stay in their seats and be watched by trained security personnel.

WE WERE DEEPLY suspicious of the experts, but we were in a fix too: Walker, smart as we knew him to be, was a weird kid, too weird for pre-school. All our attention to him wasn't getting him any better prepared for a classroom. So Ellen found a very well-regarded, very busy team of experts in Evanston—a psychologist, a psychiatrist, and an educational consultant, all women—who fitted us in a month later. The psychologist first saw Ellen and Walker together and then insisted on seeing me separately. The day before my conference with her Ellen gave me a pep talk.

"Remember to smile and act agreeable and don't argue with her too much," she said.

"You talkin' to me? There's nobody else here. You talkin' to me?" I said.

"She's nice and seems to like Walker. You might be a little put off by her sad way of talking—she talks kind of like an undertaker—but she might be able to help us."

THE NEXT DAY, smiling, jaunty of step and trusting of my fellow man, I walked into the big, bright, book-lined office of the child psychologist.

"Nice to meet you, Mr. Hughes," she said, in a friendly enough but somber way, shook my hand, and closed the door behind me.

"It's good to meet you," I replied, chipperly.

She then stood still and stared at me. There were several places to sit: a couch, a couple of easy chairs on my right, a couple of hard-backed chairs in front of me near her desk, another few around a small table off to my left. I glanced at each in turn and waited for her to indicate where she wanted me to plant myself.

But this wasn't happening. Moments passed. To avoid her stare, I glanced about the room—big windows behind the desk looking out on trees, brightly colored toys and children's books off to the side in a play area, psychology journals on a coffee table.

"This is such a pleasant office," I said.

"My, you are a curious person, aren't you?" was her reply.

"Oh, ha ha, I guess I am," I said. "Where would you like me to sit?"

"Oh, anywhere you like," she said, still bolted to her viewing stand and squinting slightly.

I thought: Is this a test? Does my choice of chair indicate something crucial about me? If I pick a comfy spot, am I a self-indulgent pleasure-seeker? If I pick a straight-backed chair, am I uptight and afraid of intimacy? If I pick a chair on the other side of the room, am I trying to hide something?

Unafraid and well-balanced, I picked a chair right in front of her desk.

Seating herself behind the desk, she asked, "Well, can you tell me about Walker? Start with his birth, and tell me how he has developed and what you think about it."

This was my kind of topic. Starting off slowly but building speed and enthusiasm as I went, I told the story of Walker's brilliance, sparkling personality, odd behavior, silence, perpetual energy, and our theories of how he was developing. I cited our favorite example, the one that matched our sky-high hopes for him—Albert Einstein. The greatest mind of the century didn't speak until the age of three, didn't talk normally until nine, and described himself as having been preoccupied as a young child with space and time.

The psychologist was listening to my rambling cultist/fanatic discourse pretty much the way our friend at the dinner table did: showing agreeableness and doubt at the same time, with a new overlay of pathos. Though she didn't speak the actual words, her stare, tilt of the head, and sympathetic nod said to me—clear as a bell—"You *poor* thing."

But I was in no "poor thing" state of mind. I was humming along.

"Walker looks at objects in a fascinating way," I said, pulling a ballpoint pen out of my pocket and holding it next to my ear. "He'll hold something, like an action figure, on the side of his head like this. Then he'll bob it up and down, sort of dance it forward while peering to the side, trying to see when it comes into view. Then he dances it in front of his face like this, follows it with his eyes, turns the plastic guy around and around, and waltzes it over to the other side of his head, watching it disappear again."

"I see," she observed, sadly. "He plays with toys in an inappropriate way."

"Well, I know it's not what another child would do with a plastic army guy, but it's interesting." To this she nodded up and down in a "yes" that meant "no." "Maybe not exactly Einstein," I said. "Maybe we'll have to settle for Stephen Hawking."

No smile. Long pause. Her eyes widened a bit, as if she suddenly realized that all along she'd been talking to a maniac. "I can see you really love your son, but I don't like what I'm hearing," she said.

She didn't buy my Portrait of the Astrophysicist as a Young Boy and wasn't buying much of anything I said except for the obvious information about the ways Walker wasn't keeping up with children his age.

A FEW WEEKS later Ellen took Walker to be tested by the other two experts, the psychiatrist and the educational consultant. We had high hopes as well as high anxiety about the IQ test. We had both read Stephen J. Gould's *The Mismeasure of Man*, which exposes the dubious history of the test and the false but widespread notion that the test measures "intelligence" as though it were a tangible "thing in the brain" and not the vague, elusive, contingent, quasi-untestable concept that it actually is.

But we knew teachers and psychologists revered the IQ score as a sort of identity tag and so we hoped that if Walker could get a high score, teachers would have less trouble getting past his silence and his arm-waving and his staring at shiny objects and see a more complicated boy.

The educational consultant brought a special sort of IQ test, one designed for the deaf, and presented it to Walker without speaking to him. "It would ruin the validity of the test," the psychiatrist told Ellen, "if we spoke to him at all."

"But Walker will find it weird not to be spoken to," Ellen said.

"This is the only way we can do the test. Walker is not oriented toward sound and auditory clues. He's a visual child," the educational consultant said. "Oh, and by the way, Mrs. Hughes, you shouldn't be in the room while we give the test."

"Oh, I'll stay," Ellen said, smiling. "I won't be in the way."

So the educational consultant, who had been a talking human a moment before, became a mime: She didn't "walk against the wind," but she pointed at blocks and gestured with her arms and fluttered her hands in Walker's face, all the while keeping her mouth shut. Thrillingly enough, Walker breezed through the various tasks —putting blocks in order, finding shapes that didn't belong with other ones, even coming up with smart but unexpected solutions to problems (such as finding novel similarities between objects). All the while Walker was doing this, Ellen noticed, he was quietly singing a Raffi song, "Numbers Rumba."

The boy was actually *having fun!*

When he had finished everything in front of him, the psychiatrist said to the educational consultant: "Why did you stop?"

She then moved her lips. "I ran out of test materials. I didn't bring the rest. I didn't expect him to get this far."

"How can we get an accurate score if we stop before he misses any questions?" Ellen asked.

"Well, Mrs. Hughes, you should be happy to know that he's not retarded. That's the main thing," the psychiatrist said, as though speaking to a child.

Then it hit Ellen: They had assumed he would do poorly! They hadn't believed anything we said about how he enjoyed puzzles, how he loved to use his mind, for they understood him at a glance better than we possibly could. They were the missionaries; we were the simple tribal people.

WE WAITED ANOTHER month for a meeting at which they'd give us their evaluation.

It was like waiting for a verdict from a jury that had scowled whenever our defense attorney had risen to speak. Ellen warned me beforehand: "Behave yourself. Don't argue with them. I know it doesn't seem likely, but they may give us some hints on how to help Walker. We want to leave them with a positive feeling about us—we might need them later for some reason."

"My lips are sealed," I said. "I'll just grin and nod like a happy idiot." Shutting up and letting Ellen do the talking became my tactical signature ever since I had exploded in the face of the Speech Lady.

And I really stuck to my resolution, even when the psychiatrist lowered the boom and scolded us: "Walker is autistic, and I'm afraid to say that autism is a lifelong condition for which there is no cure. But with early intervention and the right services, some improvement can be made. Unfortunately, you should have come to us yesterday. Walker's not getting the services he needs."

Ellen smiled and said, "Well, better late than never!" I smiled even more broadly and nodded "yes" but thought, *We did come to you "yesterday." In fact we came three months ago!*

The psychiatrist went on: "Walker's IQ is 129, so there's basic intelligence there that we can work with."

Ellen and I looked at each other, surprised to get a number that could prove helpful, and Ellen said, "That's good to know."

I smiled as though auditioning for a toothpaste commercial. *How much higher would it be if you had brought enough materials to the test? By the way, what's your IQ? I now know Walker's is above mine.*

Continuing with my sly strategy, I let Ellen return the serve when the educational consultant reiterated her pet theory: "Walker needs an educational plan based on visual stimuli since he's not oriented to auditory stimuli."

"Yes," said Ellen, nodding at this message from the mountaintop. "You've mentioned that before. What clued you to that idea?"

"I noticed that when he was playing there was a dog barking outside. Walker never raised his head or looked at the window. He just continued to pick up objects and stare at them with interest."

I continued to smile and look out the window, even though no dog was barking. *But I told you! I told you! Walker lives in one of the noisiest environments imaginable. If he responded to every loud noise, he'd be perpetually plastered to our front windows. And didn't you hear him sing, "Numbers Rumba"?*

And I let Ellen ask the main question on our minds, the one reason we had them evaluate Walker in the first place: "Do you have any suggestions about what we should do at home with Walker to prepare him for school?"

"Oh, you're doing a great job," she said, the two others shaking their heads in vigorous agreement. "Just keep doing what you've been doing. Sit with him and work on numbers and writing, but also follow his lead and go with the things he's doing. If he pushes a truck, you push one too and talk to him about it. If you're taking a walk and he wants to go in a certain direction, turn that way. Work with his interests. Build on his strengths."

"Thank you," Ellen said. "That's good to know. We'll do that—what we've been doing."

I did my best to look at our educational consultant with gratitude, humble tribesman to missionary.

Finally, I was most proud of my exit from the interview, during which I did *not* jump up and down and pull out the remaining hair on my head when the psychiatrist intoned: "Remember, Mr. and Mrs.

Hughes, you are part of the team now. Don't let anyone tell you that you aren't. You are an integral part of Walker's team." *PART of the team?! We ARE the team! We are the owners, managers and coaches. We are the pitchers, infielders and outfielders. You people can be the first and third base coaches—maybe a pitching coach—and very expendable at that.*

LATE THAT NIGHT we did our post-mortem.

"They're only interested in the things that he does that let them say he's autistic," Ellen said. "They have no interest in anything else. If something contradicts the label, they want nothing to do with it. They're just unbelievable!" She was smiling, almost laughing. "They have a lot of nerve pontificating when they know so little."

I was drinking a beer as well as drinking in her disgust. I thought, *Yes! I knew they were jerks all along!*

WHEN A MAN has some physical affliction, we decided, such as cancer or tuberculosis, people don't write him off as "cancer guy" or "TB guy." He is still considered a person with all the mystery and complexity of personhood. When a woman has schizophrenia or depression, she carries the burden of a terrible problem, but she is still a full human being. But when a child has severe autism, all bets are off. The boy or girl suddenly becomes one-dimensional.

We ever afterwards referred to "The Three Bozos," and statements like "You should have come to us yesterday" and "He is a visual child" became little in-jokes.

But we were crushed too. We had secretly hoped they'd be taken with Walker and his brilliant, puzzling, winning singularity. The word "autism" blew all his qualities away, vaporized the mystery, turned him into something simple, comprehensible, and finally boring: a boy who could be characterized with one word. It was not a pleasing augur of how he'd be received by the world.

The good thing was that we were no longer mere deluded parents. The Developmental Police had given us a number that we planned to wave like a flag. 129! On a piece of paper! With the names of experts on the letterhead!

Armed with this figure attached to our boy by the modern science of child development, we took a deep breath and approached the brave new world of public education.

SIX

Homeschooling I

Cemetery School

Ellen's first thought as Walker bit her forearm was, *God, I hope nobody sees this.*

She was standing in line with a dozen other mothers and children at a public school screening in a noisy auditorium and smiling... smiling ...smiling.

Her second thought was, *Why?* Until the little teeth sank into her flesh, her hopes had been high. Only a half hour before this, Walker was reading a book, *The Scary Old House*, loudly and with feeling. He seemed up for this. He was pumped. "School! School!" he shouted as he walked, grinning, out the front door dressed in his regulation '80s Hanna Andersen duds, a beautiful curly-haired astrophysicist at the start of his brilliant career.

And biting? He had rarely bitten either of us before. And *now*, when presentation was everything? Suddenly the proud mother was like some smuggler of wild animals at customs, bluffing and directing attention away from herself.

"Can he say his name, Mrs. Hughes?" an enormous, fat woman behind a table asked Ellen.

Seated now, the trapped lynx in her lap, Ellen found herself saying, "Well, he doesn't really say his name." Walker tugged at her blouse and squirmed. "He doesn't normally act like this. It's very strange. He must be nervous."

"Does he talk at all?" the questioner asked, staring and squinting at the wild-eyed, red-faced boy.

"He can recite the alphabet backwards and forwards, and count to 50."

"Does he say sentences?"

"Well, no," Ellen said through her teeth, smiling and wincing. "He has said very few actual sentences. But he can complete almost any line from any Gershwin song if you sing the first half." Walker wriggled out of her arms and slipped to the floor. He was now on his back, kicking. "I'm sorry. He must be very upset. Ha ha! Oh well!"

"Does he point at things?"

"Well, no, he did when he was one," Ellen said, pulling on his hands and trying to coax him back up. "But he won't anymore."

The evaluator raised her chin and like a prim teacher reprimanding a child said, "We don't say 'won't,' Mrs. Hughes. We say 'can't.'"

ELLEN WAS DEALING with too much for this remark to register until later. She just welded the smile to her face and moved on to the interview with the psychologist.

While she spoke to the psychologist, another evaluator took Walker into a room to observe him. After five minutes, the evaluator emerged with him and said, "He's too low for any program we've got."

The psychologist said, "But the mother here says he has a high IQ and can read."

"Oh, I'll have to take another look at him then."

Then a man with a briefcase bustled over and announced that he was the speech evaluator. He was thin and frail-looking and wore tight green rayon pants that were too short for him, the sort of guy, Ellen noted later, that she would feel sorry for if she saw on the street. Before he put down his briefcase and without getting more than a brief glimpse of Walker, he said, "Well, this one's obviously retarded. Let's see what else is wrong with him."

The smile melted from Ellen's face. She turned to the psychologist and said, "I'm sorry. This man isn't bright enough to evaluate my child." She then picked up our savage little lunatic and left the building.

They had been there for all of twenty-five minutes.

When she came home with Walker and related all this to me, I ricocheted around the room in frustration, inventing snappy comebacks and by and large justifying the division of duties that kept me hidden from public view.

When I calmed down, Ellen told me about her resolution to take up the psychologist on a suggestion she had made: to observe the program at a North Side school not far away that had an "excellent" pre-school class for autistic children.

A week later the pleasant director of the special education program at the school was escorting Ellen around, showing her each class one by one, and finally taking her outside to the playground where the twelve or so kids in the autism program were being supervised by two teachers. The first thing Ellen noticed, with a sinking heart, was that the fence around the playground had gaps in it, and that if our wild son were to be let loose here, he would disappear through that gap like a passenger sucked through the open door of an airplane cabin at 40,000 feet. Immediately she sensed that Walker would be considered "too low" even for this group.

"That boy over there," she said, pointing to a kid nimbly climbing a pole, "he doesn't look autistic to me."

"It's funny you mention that," she said. "We've been thinking the same thing for two years now."

Two years! Ellen thought, stunned. And he hasn't been moved to some other program yet?

"Could you describe your son a little?" the director said.

"Well, he's not verbal and wouldn't be able to swing on the swings or climb as well as some of these kids, but he's been tested to have a high IQ."

"A high IQ?" the director said, surprised. "None of these children has high intelligence." She then called one of the teachers over, introduced Ellen and described Walker.

"No," the teacher said. "This wouldn't be the place for him. All these students are retarded. They're autistic, you know."

As Ellen was leaving, she asked the director how long the pre-school program lasted each day. We were hoping to find a place that would take him three hours in the morning so she could take on more clients and get more writing done.

"Oh, don't worry, Mrs. Hughes. It's an all-day program."

This was our first invitation to dump off our presumably impossible, incurable child in all-day custodial care.

It seemed more frightening than tempting to us.

THE PROFESSIONALS WE met were mainly interested in discovering, predicting, proving and finding the jargon for Walker's limits. But it seemed to us that a Limiting Wall Theory of pedagogy was fatal. If a teacher proceeded with the idea that a wall would soon be hit—and had a predetermined idea of the exact location of that wall, its height and length and thickness and immovability—that teacher wouldn't have the heart to keep trying when faced with any resistance. If you toss a ball to an autistic kid and he doesn't throw it back, how many times will you try it again? At what point do you check off "Can't play ball" on the Master List?

Our policy was to throw the ball until we couldn't stand it any longer, take a rest, and then try again. Sometimes this worked; sometimes it didn't. Sometimes we succeeded or, more commonly, redefined success; sometimes we felt like we were about to lose our minds. But even when we flat-out failed, Walker usually let us know he loved us for trying.

One morning I sat with him at the dining room table trying, with an accelerating pulse rate, to teach addition and subtraction using a pile of pennies. This was hard work. He often swept the pennies—or plastic army men or McDonald's Happy Meals' toys or playing cards—off the table. As on several previous mornings, he didn't show much understanding, but this day he kept at it like a trooper despite my impatience. I pointed at two groups of pennies. "Now Walker, tell me, five pennies and three pennies are . . ." I moved the groups together and started counting them: "One, two, three . . . " He leaned over the coins, smiling broadly at them like they were old friends, his face just inches from the surface of the table, and whispered distinctly, "This is wonderful."

Moments like this kept us going and convinced us that we—ourselves, the parents in denial—should take charge.

We decided to become homeschoolers.

"HOMESCHOOLING," ELLEN AND I would always say to anyone who asked, "is not our cup of tea."

For me, it was far less than my cup of tea; it was actually repellent. I loved school, that is, "real" institutional school. All my childhood, pleasing the teacher was my constant study. Was a volunteer needed to clean the erasers after school? Why, that's me, Sister! Was an altar boy needed at 6:30 mass and a patrol boy for the street corner at 7:15? Why, that's me too, Sister! And staying in school as long as I could was my life's goal. After getting a Ph.D., I got a college teaching job which gave me a career that positioned me in the juvenile environment I so loved.

Ellen, too, recalled being such a good student that the teachers hardly knew she was there. So as homeschoolers we—and I far more than Ellen—felt more like outlaws than many other parents would.

This criminal feeling was enhanced by a phone call Ellen received a few weeks after the public school evaluation. It was the principal of the school where Ellen had escaped with her wild cat of a son.

"Mrs. Hughes," the principal told her, "you haven't completed Walker's evaluation. You need to make an appointment to have him officially placed in a program."

"Oh, we've decided to teach him at home," Ellen told her.

"OK, but when he's seven we'll be coming to get you," she said, menacingly. "You can't hide."

When Ellen told me about this threat, I couldn't believe it.

I laughed. "No! She didn't actually use the words, 'We'll be coming to get you'?"

"Those were her words," Ellen assured me.

"Come on—'You can't hide' ?"

"I know it's hard to believe, but I remember exactly."

Though I pretended it was all very hilarious, those words vibrated in my head like like the "Dum-da-dum-dum" of the old "Dragnet" TV show. For Ellen these were fighting words to begin a personal crusade. After all, homeschooling is legal in Illinois and increasingly popular. If the school system was going to give up on our son, surely we could do better.

I knew all this rationally, but it took me years to accept the fact that Ellen and I weren't Butch Cassidy and the Sundance Kid trailed by a posse of truant officers.

Ellen pointed out that even if authorities came and examined our methods, they'd see that the entire interior of our house resembled a pre-school and they would probably be very impressed with the book-shelves in the living room filled with children's books and the educational posters and maps on the walls. Our idea of dining room art was a poster of "Snakes of North America." On the wall near the stereo was a full-length mirror for Walker to stare at himself while he danced.

As child-worshipping cultists, we were already homeschoolers. We were just lucky that we were in a position to continue doing it. I arranged my schedule so I could teach in the evenings while Ellen wrote in the mornings. Of course, she couldn't take on anything like the number of freelance jobs that she would have liked, and so a vast ditch of financial debt grew deeper and wider by the year. If not for the generous checks sent by Ellen's mother each month—amounting to the cost of tuition at a good pre-school—anxiety about money would have swamped us.

ACCORDING TO THE literature, some homeschoolers actively try to duplicate some of the features of a public school. They ring a bell, sit down at 8:30 each weekday morning and have a regulation-style lesson: "Now, Jeremy, give me that spitball and sit up straight and look at the blackboard." (Do they pay gangbangers to visit their backyards in the afternoon to try to sell the children drugs during recess?) Many more homeschoolers, of course, take advantage of the greater flexibility of their schedules to teach in more creative ways geared to the specific abilities of the child.

But Walker posed a special problem: What were his "basics"? We decided that our short-term goal was simply to coax him toward the normal. So homeschooling, for us, meant getting Walker out of the home as much as possible. Out he went to dance classes, occupational therapy sessions, speech classes, swimming classes, reading tutorials. Out he went to museums and parks and malls while we chattered to him about everything we saw.

One of Walker's most mystifying traits was a complete absence of acquisitiveness. We assumed that to be a normal kid in America was to want *stuff*, lots of it. But Walker was strangely uninterested in consumerism, especially for a so-called "object-oriented" boy. By his third Christmas, he wouldn't open any gifts. He wouldn't even begin to unwrap a present on his birthday. He just played with the first toy presented to him and ignored all the rest. He did learn to love many things we bought for him—he would sit by the hour and page through a book while playing the accompanying audiotape; he enjoyed Hot Wheels and toy trains; he revered anything given to him by his Uncle Pete—but he would show very little *initial* interest in anything.

A core nightmare for most parents is the child in the shopping cart in Toys "R" Us pointing at some pricey, colorful piece of plastic and screaming "Gimme!" But this awful situation is at bottom reassuringly normal. Pointing, gazing at the bright things all around and verbally expressing desire for them are all part of the process of a young person learning to have an identity, insisting on a self and changing the immediate environment to suit the self. The reverse situation is far scarier. Walker, wheeled through a toy store, did not point, did not verbalize, did not *look*. In fact, his failure to talk seemed closely related to his failure to point, to hit a wooden peg with a wooden hammer, to sing a song loud enough to be easily heard, to *assert* himself confidently in his world.

So we called it "Greed 101" and took him regularly to toy stores and malls and supermarkets. We picked up pints of ice cream, bags of frozen french fries, Speak 'n' Say toys, Fisher-Price recorders, cartoon videos, stories on audiotape, put them in front of his eyes and talked about them like museum docents on speed.

I'd say, "Wow, get a load of all these books, Walker."

He looks in the opposite direction.

"See this one, man?"

I open up a book about trucks, and put it in front of his face.

"Can you believe the wheels on this thing! They're as big as a house! Look how small the man looks next to them!"

Walker shows no interest. I buy the book.

We wanted him to look, to talk, to point—to show desire in some way. Any expressed interest, we knew, could be an educational goal we could pursue with vigor.

ONE DAY IN August I was homeschooling him hard. I had tried printing with him, and he did write a few words—"elephant," "telephone," "Cookie Monster"—but after only ten minutes he refused to go on. Then I tried reading with him, but he wouldn't do this at all. Then I threw his favorite, enormous, red rubber ball to him, he caught it and tossed it over my head over the side of the balcony and it smashed a big wooden bowl in the kitchen.

Then, despite the foul mood I had worked myself into, I perversely started to work on my Binary Project.

"Walker, what would you like to do? Go to the park?

No answer as he jumped in an agitated way in the corner of the dining room.

"To the zoo?"

No answer.

"Walker, what's better, the zoo or the park?"

No answer. Not even a look my way.

This nonconversation went on for an excruciating time until Ellen and Davy came in the door.

"What's going on?" Ellen asked, seeing the state I was in.

"I'm trying to get Walker to tell me what he'd prefer doing, going to a park or going to the zoo. Goddammit, it's driving me crazy."

"I don't think he cares, really," Ellen said. "They're the same to him."

Then Walker, in a quiet, high, soft voice said distinctly: "No they're not. They're very different."

Ellen and I looked at each other like people who had seen a ghost but doubted the evidence of their eyes. Our faces registered a silent *My God, it's really happening.*

Ellen then said, as matter-of-factly as she could, "Walker, that's great talking! So which is better? What do you like better, the park or the zoo?"

Walker beamed at us with pride, but said nothing, absolutely nothing more.

Wonderful, mysterious, inexplicable blips of smooth sentences came out of the blue like this from time to time, and they always gave us great hope. But we could never interest anyone else in them. We'd mentioned them to three different doctors, his (so far) two speech teachers, and the occupational therapist he had begun seeing, but since none of them had ever heard him say anything so complex, and the idea itself didn't jibe with the assumed pervasiveness of autism, they discounted it.

One afternoon we saw for the first time an old cartoon about a man who had a frog that sang and danced like Al Jolson. He wanted to put on concerts starring the frog and make a fortune. But whenever he put the frog in front of people, it became an inert, very froggy frog. We laughed and laughed, clutching our sides, tears streaming down our faces. It was our life.

THOUGH I WANTED to be a big, brave, unconventional teacher, it was hard for me to get out of the mindset of sitting at a table and doing a task with him, despite the fact that he often resisted this mightily. Besides, sitting was my forte. As a consequence, creative ideas often came by sheer accident, had to hit me over the head as it were, before I recognized them.

Cemetery school was one of these.

One day not long after his stunning speech about the park versus the zoo, Walker and I were driving back from an errand along Western Avenue. A Chevy Blazer was inches behind our rear bumper, the driver talking on a cell phone, flashing his lights and hoping I would somehow vaporize. "Screw you," I mumbled under my breath. At that moment Walker started to kick in his car seat behind me and go "Ah, ah, ah, ah"—a sound that to me had become like a spike through the skull.

On an impulse I turned into Rose Hill Cemetery, a place I'd driven past a hundred times before but known only from the outside as a high brick wall, a sort of prison for trees, that stretched for a mile along the busy street.

What we saw on the other side of the wall was starkly different from the world of SUVs and car dealerships and 7-Elevens and gas stations outside. Inside, everywhere we looked, were big, sweeping oaks and elms and maples, picturesque monuments, little unpretentious lakes, Canadian geese and quiet. And there was no traffic: no ticked-off drivers, no semis, no tailgaters and no impatience—in the car or out of it.

I felt my pulse decelerate, my grip on the steering wheel ease up. Walker stopped kicking and whining and stared out the window. Slowing to 15 m.p.h. and opening all the windows, I navigated the winding roads with no purpose other than to let the atmosphere waft over us. Birds chirped. Geese honked. Leaves rustled. We saw a coyote—a coyote!—run into a stand of trees. We weren't in Chicago anymore.

The next day I came back with both boys and our boom box (our car had no tape player) and we listened to story tapes and took in the scenery for a full hour, the three of us perfectly content. Books that were rejected when I tried to read them aloud myself—*The Wind in the Willows*, *The Secret Garden*, *Stuart Little*, *Charlotte's Web*, *The Chronicles of Narnia*, as well as various mind-rattling Disney productions—were received much better in the car. As the days, weeks and months passed, I tried out various kinds of music—oldies rock, baroque, even opera arias—as well as some adult books that were received well, by Patrick O'Brian and James Herriott.

Strapped into his car seat, Walker became quiet and responsive to the stories. I could see him react to scenes in the books just as I saw him react to scenes in videos. When he heard a passage he especially liked, his eyes would widen, he'd smile, he'd put his fingers in his ears and look out the window. Though silent most of the time, he clearly was getting something from the books, but exactly how much was impossible to measure. He had discriminating tastes and knew how to reject material he didn't want. Like his mother and his brother, he had a tragically sad intolerance for my Jack Benny radio tapes. ("Ellen, just listen to this one little part where Rochester buys a tie for Jack. You'll love it! Really!"). But he did develop a thing for bluegrass music while cruising around what an uncle of mine used to call "the marble orchard."

The place itself was a bucolic image of the city outside the walls. There were the rich neighborhoods of mini-mansion-mausoleums and towering obelisks. There were the middle class neighborhoods of small, flat, innocuous slabs. There were ethnic neighborhoods—the Asian section was growing and vast. And then there were the people: the Diva (a statue of a reclining mother and child in a large glass box); the CEO (a statue of Mr. Leonard Wells Volk d. 1895, seated and taking a break from a long journey); the War Hero (a big rock memorializing General Thomas, the Rock of Chickamauga); and their pets (twin statues of large Dobermans and one of a full-size stag).

In his book *Lincoln at Gettysburg*, Garry Wills notes that Rose Hill was built during the "rural cemetery movement" of the nineteenth century. Beautiful cemetery parks like Rose Hill and Gettysburg (designed by the same landscape architect) were meant to elevate the human spirit, even educate visitors in virtue, because communing with nature in itself provided a "school for the living."

Of course, the original proponents of rural cemeteries didn't imagine a father and his mentally disabled son tooling around in an Escort at Christmas time, gazing at the heavy snow in the tree branches, fumbling with a boom box and listening to the story of Ratty and Moley sharing a holiday glass of mulled ale in *The Wind in the Willows*. Their ideas were grander than that.

But I like to think there was a certain symmetry of intentions, and that our strange schoolhouse was something they would have endorsed.

Walker, age 3, and a friend

ANOTHER UNCONVENTIONAL TEACHING "method"—my crowning achievement as a homeschooling educator in fact—was running. This too was a discovery I only stumbled onto by accident, but once made, it proved to be a godsend, for both Walker and me.

SEVEN

Homeschooling II

Running With Walker

It wasn't "running," exactly.

What Walker did was *like* running the way a circus trapeze act is like gymnastics or stunt flying is like airline travel—that is, it was similar, but it was so much more.

Take the liftoff. Beginning on tiptoe at the bottom of our front stairs, he'd turn and face the "Tragically Hip" store straight ahead, a block away on Belmont. Lowering his left heel flat on the sidewalk while stomping hoe-down style with his right, he'd pump his arms up and down and do a scary "booga-booga" shake of his hands in the air; he'd tilt his head back, grin in an open-mouthed way suitable for rapid oxygen intake, open his eyes wide, and give me a look that seemed to say, "Now *this* is what I was born to do!" He'd then spring skyward and forward, as if his destination were as much vertical as horizontal, and become as airborne as an earthbound seven-year-old boy could be.

His heels seldom touched the ground. He was skipping, but moving ahead so fast that it never seemed quite like skipping in any normal sense of the word. It was "trick-skipping" or "skip-sprinting" or "sprint-dancing," but it wasn't exactly "running."

And his nimbleness about it all was astonishing. Ice, cracks in the sidewalk, gravel, grass, hidden ruts in open fields, wind, rain, mothers with strollers, bicyclists, rollerbladers, homeless people, men stretched out for a nap on the sidewalk—he sped lightly over, in, among, and around all. He was like a happy-go-lucky barnstorming pilot; every difficulty was a challenge. He could skip uphill and downhill and, most impressively, *backwards* uphill. His progress was never predictably straight. In mid-skip, he'd twist suddenly to the right or left, ditching me momentarily while I jogged on straight ahead. He could stop so abruptly that he seemed free of the law of momentum and skip instantly backwards, sending me turning and tripping and otherwise making a spectacle of myself.

He could do all this on frigid winter mornings in Lincoln Park Zoo; on narrow slippery sidewalks in mid-winter with snow piled boy-high on both sides of him; past sun worshipper-gazers at North Avenue Beach and human gridlock at Taste of Chicago. He was energized by running in the open air, freed by it.

And so was I.

WE DISCOVERED THE liberating power of the Great Outdoors on a miserably hot day in late September of our homeschooling "first grade."

At 11:30 that morning, I was already losing my patience. Ellen and Davy had left the house, and I wanted to do some math with Walker, so I'd gotten out a picture workbook from our large stash of such items and sat at the dining room table with him. The book was asking us about the numerical-digital consequences of pilfering a single balloon from a clown who had three balloons in his grasp.

"So, man, what's 3 take away 1?" I said with phony good cheer. I was hot, uncomfortable and irritated because I was pretty sure that he would not answer the question but rather get up and dash down the hall, just as he had done on my four previous tries in the last fifteen minutes.

And—I *knew* it! *Just* as I expected!—he closed the book, roughly pushed his chair back, and took off.

I needed a break. So I put on Walker's favorite videotape, one I knew would occupy him for a while, "Walt Disney Sing-Along Songs: Bare Necessities," and I sat down to grade my papers for the class I was teaching that night.

This was a mistake for two reasons. First, "Bare Necessities." Most young children are capable of re-playing a video until the parents grind their teeth at the sound of it, but Walker, the child with special needs, had rewound this tape until it had been sledge-hammered into my frontal lobe. The reverberating sound of Phil Harris's voice and the image of Baloo the Bear in my head threatened to keep me awake each night when I went to bed. If not for the mighty effort I made to fall asleep by force-fantasizing about pitching no-hitters in Wrigley Field, the entire twenty-five minute videotape would have replayed in my brain, in color, in real time, every single night.

The second reason was that, though I loved teaching my classes, I would have rather gnawed my own arm off than grade student essays. I'd let anything distract me from reading them. I'd sit down with a clipboard full of papers, red ball point in hand, look at the first paper, and realize I had to vacuum the carpet, wash the bathroom floor, or read yesterday's comic strips.

In this case, I opted to pick on Walker.

I was sitting in my L. L. Bean "Kennedy rocking chair" pretending to think about the essays, but I was in no presidential frame of mind. I kept looking up to check out what Walker was doing, or rather, not doing. He was making no progress through the tape. After the first three songs or so, he'd rewind the tape to the beginning. It was always important to see the tape from before the actual start every time—every logo, every advertisement. The brilliant autistic writer Donna Williams talks of "intros and exits," how she was obsessed with the start of anything and the end of anything. So too with Walker. If he missed the FBI Warning, whatever he saw afterwards simply did not count. If he missed the end credits, his day was ruined, and ours too.

So I started in on him. "Walker, you've seen this section of the tape way too many times. I'm going to have to take the VCR away now." This was his signal to wail and jump at me and tear at my shirt. I peeled him off me and disconnected the VCR. "Here, you can watch any TV show you like." I turned on Cartoon Network. "Or you can listen to some of your tapes." I pointed to his tape player over on the dining room table.

I sat down again with my papers, but I knew what I had to do. I watched him.

He then looked up at the small front window high in the gable of the arched ceiling. He was looking at the sun and walking back and forth into and out of the square on the rug where the beam of light hit the floor.

"No!" I shouted at him, leaped up and grabbed him by the shoulders. "Don't look at the sun. You'll go blind. Do you understand me? You'll...go...BLIND!"

I then got out a ladder, climbed up to the window, and scotch-taped black construction paper on it. But as I did this Walker was already seeking the light at the front door, four feet to the right of the base of my ladder, peering at the sun through the four tiny windows in the top of the door. He walked on tiptoe back and forth looking through each window in turn, his arms raised, his hands waving so rapidly they seemed just a blur.

I raced down the ladder. I got out more construction paper. Sweating, yelling at him, and generally storming around, I cut the pieces to fit the windows and stuck them in place while the "Looney Toons" theme from the television created a soundtrack for the afternoon. I was Porky Pig, steaming and fretting, unable to contain the Wascally Wabbit who always found a new way to torment me—but nobody was laughing.

A half hour later, when I had built a "Les Miserables"-style barricade out of chairs and end tables to keep him away from the front door and had effectively cut off all direct sunlight into the room, I sat down in a heap in my presidential rocking chair to view my handiwork.

There stood Walker in the dining room, undefeated, pacing forwards and backwards, staring excitedly at a McDonald's Happy Meal toy on the table. The great demon Repetition still had him in thrall.

And there I rocked, looking at him, completely out of my mind.

Suddenly I had an uncharacteristic burst of sanity. "Walker, let's get out of here," I said. "Let's go to the zoo."

For the first time that day, he spoke: "Zoo! Zoo! Shoes and socks!"

Our normal zoo trips were athletic affairs, but they had, over many months, become less fun and even stress-filled. We'd begin, him skip-running and I jogging, at the Lincoln Park Conservatory at the far north end of the zoo. Always, always, I let him lead me wherever he wished. Other six-year-olds could tell their parents, ad nauseam, exactly what they wanted and where they wanted to go every minute of the day. Since Walker couldn't do this, I figured the least I could do is let him vote with his feet.

Usually we covered the entire length of Lincoln Park Zoo, north to south, doubling back and re-tracing our steps often, much *too* often. By age six the zoo had already ceased to be a mere zoo for him. Through the magic of free admission, it had morphed into a sort of fantastic back yard. As a toddler in a stroller, he drove Ellen and me nuts with his refusal actually to look at the animals. In the dark ape house, inches from the glass wall of the gorilla habitat, Ellen and I would crouch down on either side of Walker's stroller and say, "Walker, look! A gorilla!" But Walker would repeat his passing fire engine routine of looking up, down, or away, even when the gorilla leaped and body-slammed the glass where we stood.

But in a slow evolution over many trips, Walker eased up and started to look at the animals, had regular stops with particular friends—the baby elephant, the penguins, the tiger, the sea lions—until he evolved past staring into the sheer release of running through the zoo itself. He attacked curves, ramps, stairs, the sidewalk at the edge of the lagoon, the path past the Viking ship, with wide-eyed zest. Both boys loved the place and for a time—like the summer of Walker's big seizure—they did a good impression of normal brothers there hanging out with their dad.

But Walker insisted on traveling farther and farther and more and more eccentrically. He'd leave the barn at the Farm in the Zoo and then have to return. He'd go under the bridge at the lagoon and then have to skip backwards under it again—and again. He'd seem to make great progress in a direct line from the elephants to the zebras and then—maddeningly—insist on retracing his steps. Davy, understandably, had no tolerance for this and had none of Walker's outrageous stamina; he had more productive things to do with his time.

So the zoo had changed over time from Walker's huge, personal playground to a trap, yet another place where Repetition pushed him, and thus me, willy-nilly, hither and yon. Sometimes, to break the spell of going into and out of the small mammal habitat (as with a video-tape, a classic "intro" problem), I'd have to pick him up bodily and take him out to the parking lot. Sometimes I'd break his Sisyphean route up and down the ramp to the underwater sea lion habitat by getting behind him, grabbing his arms and pushing him forward while rapidly chattering in his ear about the wonderful places we were headed.

But on this oddly hot September afternoon, with a soothing "cooler-near-the-lake" breeze in our faces, he did something very different. He left the chicken house at the far south end of the zoo and instead of his habitual route—backing up to the chickens again or going left to see the horses—he turned to the right, through a gate, and *out of the zoo!*

I had two thoughts: (a) What's up? but more importantly, (b) How wonderful! Liberty! Euphoria! Released from the crazy maze the zoo had become for us as well as the madness of the living room of an hour ago, we were out and we were moving—straight ahead, no backtracking or stopping to tag up with trees or tapping fence posts with our feet or running backwards to press our backs up against lampposts. The sky, the trees, the very dips and rises of the blacktop path were all new and vivid. The old park was suddenly, inexplicably, a wonderland to explore.

Walker, age 15, on the El platform near our house

We found ourselves on the lakefront running south toward Oak Street Beach. To our right, men were playing chess, couples were sitting on the cement ledge, and beyond them was the vast wall of apartment buildings facing the lake and beginning to cast one huge shadow across the Drive. Bicyclists and rollerbladers and runners sped past us and toward us—a young woman with a blonde ponytail and a big smile race-walked toward us, flashed a smile at Walker and said, "*Somebody's* happy!" The last of the year's sunbathers were scattered on the sand to our left and white sails spotted the blue lake beyond.

"Look ahead, Walker," I said. "See the big building that has X's on it? That's called the John Hancock Building." Walker actually looked at it and smiled. "And see that building that says 'The Drake'? That's where my mom and dad, Grandma Ruth and Grandpa Bob, had their honeymoon." Walker looked where I pointed and smiled.

Repetition, the Demon that possessed him in the house, seemed to have limited powers over him on this day, out in the open air. And it was hard for me to feel anxiety or anger or hopelessness with him skip-running along beside me, flirting with speeding passersby, checking out the scenery, enjoying his city. From the pitched battle of a few hours ago we had transformed ourselves into a father and son who were in sync, in harmony, on the same page, transmitting at the same wavelength.

We had a new identity: we were runners.

FROM THAT DAY running became The Thing We Do. I planned, if pressed about it by inquiring minds, to nod sagely and furrow my brow and indicate that of course it was part of a shrewd homeschooling regimen.

But in fact I had no pedagogic goal at all. We ran because it was fun, got us out of the house and out of our tense heads. We looked at things and people and thought about *them*, not our problems. I'd talk to him—sometimes nonstop—about the things we saw. I'd spot what he seemed to be looking at and say something about it. Or I'd point out things—traffic, clouds, advertisements, ice on the lake, architecture—and give mini-lectures. But I felt more like a normal father chatting with his normal kid and answering his questions (though Walker never asked any) than like the anxious would-be Mr. Chips I was in the house.

Over the next several months Walker devised many routes up and down the lakefront. There was the Southern Trajectory—the Number 22 Clark Street bus down to Armitage, then over to the zoo, down the lakefront to the Water Tower, then over to the subway back home. There was the Northern Arc—from Belmont up to Waveland Golf Course, then west through Lake View to our house. There was the Great Circle Route—over to the lake, up and down the beaches and then back home.

He had a navigator's interest in where he was, stopping to look both ways before deciding on a route, smiling at familiar landmarks, going off on new routes that built on what he was already familiar with. Ellen gave him *Above Chicago*, a beautiful coffee table book of aerial photographs of the city, and he devoured it every night in bed. He'd turn the pages, spot something he recognized, smile, put his fingers in his ears, and stare wide-eyed at the picture. He knew what Lincoln Park and Michigan Avenue and Belmont Harbor looked like from the ground; this book showed him the same terrain from the sky.

His slogan could have been "location, location, location." His was the lost traveler's question—"Where am I?"—with this difference: a tourist paging through Fodor's and discovering where the museum is might smile, but he generally won't grin in delight, put his fingers in his ears, yell "Ah! Ah! Ah! Ah!" and radiate rapture.

Walker was finding things out, but he was celebrating too.

OF COURSE, NOT all father-son runs could repeat the cosmic zing of that first day. The biggest problem was that whenever we set out from home, I never knew exactly what his limit for that day would be. He perpetually ran all-out, as fast as he could, with no idea of pacing himself. We'd go and go for an hour until we were far from a bus stop, the car, the house, and he would without warning become too tired or cold or hot or bored and demand to be home—not *go* home, but actually *be* there, impossibly, like a transported crew member on "Star Trek." He'd go so far, so much farther than I imagined, that it seemed he could go on forever. Then the abrupt stop, the shriek of "HOME!" and the panicky tearing at me—his street theater scene of a boy being abused or kidnapped by an awful man, sometimes in a crowd, sometimes in stores or museums.

The snow was falling hard one morning in mid-March, in big wet flakes, driven at a steep angle by the wind off the lake. The two of us were on the pedestrian bridge over Lake Shore Drive at North Avenue and despite the blizzard we were doing fine. Today we paused to take in the thrill of the blowing snow, the *whoosh* of the tires, the wind in our faces, the transformed world around us.

Suddenly he shouted "HOME!" My heart sank; the car was parked about a half mile away.

"OK, Walker, let's get going."

"HOME! Spaghetti!" he yelled without moving.

"You're hungry? Good, let's get going. We have to get to the car first."

"Spaghetti! HOME!" Again, he didn't budge. "BACKY BACKS!"

No! I thought. *No! No!* This was the way he requested/demanded piggyback rides. Though he was a big seven years old, I still gave him regular rides on my back. I reasoned: He can't talk to me, can't communicate complex wishes, doesn't seem to understand what I say to him much of the time. Maybe sustaining the easy physical affection of toddlerhood will keep up the bond we have, help him to know he's loved despite his lack of speech.

But backy backs was also a trap I'd created for myself. This day it would mean hoisting him and then lugging him off the bridge through the driving snow to the car at the far end of the long skulling lagoon—completely out of the question. So a long terrible march ensued: pull the boy forward, peel him off my neck, shout at him to stop shouting, break his passive resistance by pulling him up off the ground, tug him forward again.

It was negative homeschooling of a searing sort, one of those moments I wondered, how bad could Special Ed be?

ON A LOVELY spring day at the south end of Lincoln Park, Walker and I were going along in our fashion: I was jogging, Walker was skip-leaping with his fingers in his ears and grinning. Three young men between eighteen and twenty-two or so approached us from the opposite direction and one of them pointed at Walker and laughed. He started to mimic Walker; then one of his pals joined in. Soon all three were skip-leaping with their fingers in their ears. Instantly furious— despite the fact that such open mockery is very rare—I made an effort to ignore them. I thought, *Don't stoop to their level, Bob.* As they passed I smiled at Walker, then looked ahead. When they were behind us I said: "Those guys are jerks, Walker. Don't let them bother you."

But deep in my brain I was busy stooping to their level as fast as I could. I started inventing put-downs that would leave them feeling guilty about their behavior and their puny worthless selves. *That's really big of you pathetic little twits, mocking a handicapped child.* [pregnant pause] *Have a nice day!*

Ever the English teacher, I wasn't satisfied with this. As we passed the statue of Abraham Lincoln I worked on my scathing speech some more. I decided my first draft wasn't sarcastic enough. *Very clever, gentlemen. It takes really big men to mock a disabled child.* [Longer, more threatening pause. They think, Will he hurt us?] *Have a nice day!*

I was satisfied with this for a moment or two, but somehow it lacked real bite. The "Have a nice day," I decided, was terrific, but there was something wrong. By now we were in front of the Cardinal's mansion and Walker was jubilant: smiling, looking at the Victorian redbrick many-chimneyed extravaganza with great pleasure. He probably expected me to say something about it as I usually did, but I had my work cut out for me.

Too wordy, I concluded. Better just to stop in front of the punks, hold Walker's hand, and stare at them until they look at me in stunned fright. Then pause a few moments, smile a little half smile, and say, *Have a nice day.*

How perfect! I thought. That's the ticket! But still…

As we rounded the corner and passed the International College of Surgeons on the inner drive, I was again fussing with my draft. Walker was smiling at the huge statue of a noble surgeon gallantly lifting a sick man, only today the good doctor was sporting two pigeons on his head. But I was full of one thought: the joy of putting those creeps in their place with the brilliant sting of my sarcasm.

I'll teach 'em to mess with an English professor!

We made our way to Chicago and State, a very long distance for us, and down the stairs to the subway platform. After a few minutes Walker got tired of waiting, or maybe my obsessed mood had finally become too much for him. He started yelling and attacking me, trying to bite my hand and flailing around. This had happened before on subway platforms and it always drove me nuts: the danger of falling onto the tracks, the amplified sound of his shouting, the alarm on the faces of the waiting passengers, the need for me to pretend to be in control—it was all more than I could deal with.

While I wrestled with him I heard a deep voice shout: "WHAT'S THE MATTER WITH HIM?" It didn't sound like the voice of help. It was a new tone to me, something like belligerent curiosity. Somebody actually expected me to carry on a shouting conversation about Walker's condition! As I struggled with Walker, again I heard: "I'm TALKING to you! I SAID, What's the MATTER with him!"

Standing behind Walker now, pinning his arms behind him and pushing his head down, I muttered: "None of your business."

"WHA'D YOU SAY!" the voice bellowed, this time with straight belligerent belligerence.

Then I saw him. He was built like an NFL lineman, slightly taller than I and a good forty pounds heavier. He was dressed in a dirty army fatigue jacket and dirty black sweatshirt and he was walking rapidly toward us. "WHA'D YOU SAY? NOBODY TALKS TO ME LIKE THAT!" For some reason my exquisite put-down—"Have a nice day!"—did not spring to my lips. I seized Walker's hand and ran with him, yanking him up the stairs: "Let's go, man! Go…go…go!" while the angry voice echoed up from the tunnel below.

When we got through the turnstile, up another flight of steps and back out on the street, I saw to my relief that he hadn't followed us. (It's one thing to kill a guy, apparently, but another to pay train fare twice in order to do it.) Walker was in a completely different mood, laughing and relaxed. I started laughing too.

I made a resolution: *Bob, from this moment on, you will control your anger. You will not obsess about people who annoy you. You will be happy in your heart, for Walker's sake and for your own.*

And for the next day or so, that was precisely what I did.

DESPITE THE OCCASIONAL dip into hell, running was wonderful. It wasn't "educational," but as Ellen would say, it was educational-*ish*. We couldn't point to anything learned by Walker in his daily expeditions through the city. No test could elicit reassuring data for the Developmental Police about how his knowledge was expanding. But as we often reminded ourselves in our late-night parent-teacher conferences, Who really knows how a kid like Walker learns? Maybe he was taking in much of what we told him and comprehending much of what he saw. Nobody could prove that he wasn't. Nobody could photograph his brain and show that the files weren't there.

We were willing to bet that the outdoor expeditions would bear fruit in the future—they certainly were helping to keep him smiling for now. I could look at his face as he ran beside me in the Loop and on the lakefront, skipped down side streets and alleys, or hiked through the deep snow of a park, and I could bask in his joyful response to the world myself. It was this picture, the face of a normal, happy boy, that I tried to keep before my mind at all times. To me this boy was just as real as that other boy, the one who got trapped in repetitions of all kinds and ached to escape.

EIGHT

The Two Walkers

There they were, four letters in upper-case, size 18 New York font with irregular spacing that seven-year-old Walker had just typed on our Macintosh: "F...U...C...K."

I stared at the screen. Was this random, like a hundred monkeys typing "Hamlet"?

Walker then touched the screen, said "Fuck!" loud and clear, turned to me and said "Fuck!" again.

My God! He was asking me a question! About something a normal kid his age would ask about! And spelling a word correctly that he had never seen in print!

We'd just returned from Sunday school where Ellen and I had taught Walker's class. (Or rather, one of us taught the class while the other "assisted" Walker, who seemed to pay little attention to what was going on.) As soon as we got home he dashed over to the computer, and this was the first thing he wrote.

Where had he heard the word? At Sunday school? Certainly not from Ellen or me. During playtime? Possibly, but the kids were never far away. Was it at the school the previous year where Ellen followed him around like a shadow? In our neighborhood while walking down the street? I know I had, I think I had, with a mighty effort, eliminated that word and a few other key terms from my working vocabulary.

Well, I thought, there it was—a miracle!

"Good talking, Walker!" I said and gave him a big hug. "Great writing. Yes, 'f' 'u' 'c' 'k'. Great spelling."

My mind raced with the possibilities. I imagined a whole system based on this word. Could he learn to say *fück* for "yes" and *fück* for "no"? Could he indicate whole questions and answers by repeating the word in a sequence with rising and falling intonation?

To answer his question I fumbled around saying how people use this word sometimes when they're angry. Walker seemed to listen to me, but I had no idea how much he actually understood, for he didn't nod "yes" or say anything else in reply. He just looked back at the screen and smiled.

He had clearly picked up on the fact that the word was special and rare and emotionally charged. Didn't this suggest that he knew much, much more about the language he heard?

I wasn't going to say anything just then to discourage him from saying it. As far as I was concerned he could say "Fuck you, Dad" all day long.

"Where did you hear the word?" I asked him. He smiled and seemed proud to have gotten this much through to me. "Who said it, Walker?" He just turned to me and looked back at the word in front of him.

"Well, that's a terrific start," I said. "Let's write some more words."

Our spontaneous writing session from that point went on as it usually did. Walker wrote "elephant" and "ambulance" and "telephone" and a dozen or so more nouns and repeated them aloud. I introduced new ones to spell and cheered him on.

But the miracle led nowhere. As in the "No it's not. It's very different" episode, he had pushed through the outside of the envelope and then slipped right back inside, never to use the word or ask about it again.

THIS WAS ANOTHER memorable and very rare appearance by the boy I'd come to think of as Walker the Regular Kid. Flashy, extraordinary, inexplicable occasions such as this one were causes for celebration. I'd note them on the Audubon calendar in the hallway in tiny near-illegible handwriting: "W. said 'fuck' today/seemed to ask what word meant/a terrific day!" For the next entry I'd write something like, "W. very agitated/ seemed upset—rather distant." Then there would be a line through the next several days with a note above it: "W. stalled/happy but quiet." Then for the next couple of weeks I wouldn't have the heart to write anything at all.

There was another apparition of the Regular Kid several weeks after the f-word lesson. We had just finished running through North Park Nature Center—a beautiful square mile or so of "real" nature "untouched" by human hands with a wide circular footpath winding through it—and we were feeling very proud of ourselves.

Making this circuit was a great achievement. The first two or three times I tried to take him into the Center, Walker got out of the car, went through the entrance, and then refused to step on the path. Then the next few times he ran along the path twenty-five, then fifty, then a hundred yards, but then turned around and insisted on getting back into the car. This cold day in November, after a dozen or so trips stretching over the previous several months, he actually completed the circuit with me—running and skipping, never, ever walking.

Afterwards we were sitting at a picnic table behind the small nature museum, an attractive brick house at the entrance. I had tried talking to him from time to time during our run. As usual, unembarrassed by my ignorance of any facts about them, I'd chattered on about the trees and birds ("Boy, look at that tree, Walker. It's so big and kind of scary looking! Ooooo!"), but he seemed intent only on completing the circuit, which was fine with me. Sitting across the table from him I did what I often did after trying and failing at conversation: I sang.

> "I've been workin' on the railroad,
> all the livelong day.
> I've been workin' on the railroad,
> Just to pass the time away."

Walker smiled and blushed, looked into my eyes and put his fingers in his ears. Then he looked down at the table, and said distinctly in his high, sweet, seldom-heard voice: "Why are you singing that song, Daddy?"

He asked this so casually, so off-handedly—as though he'd been conversing all his life—that it took a couple of seconds for the wave of astonishment to knock me down. I reached over the table and rubbed his arm. "Hey, I know you like 'Workin' On the Railroad.' It's one of our favorites." He blushed some more.

I sang on, right through "Fee, fie, fiddly-i-o," louder this time, and I talked about trains and banjos, trying hard to catch this moment and inch it forward a little. Then it occurred to me that perhaps he was embarrassed and might think the song was too babyish for a big seven-year-old guy such as himself. So I tried another song, "Isn't It a Lovely Day?" from his Fred Astaire period, and he seemed to enjoy it, but no more words, not one.

That was it. He had spoken. It was time to rest for a few more weeks.

WALKER'S OTHER SELF—the Special Needs Child—was of course the persona that he displayed to us and to the rest of the world most of the time. This was the boy who not only spoke little but wouldn't point or gesture and only typed the words on the computer keyboard that others suggested to him. He was the boy who preferred staring at light and waving his arms back and forth to playing a game with another child. He was the boy who preferred, if videos were thrust upon him, to watch only ones he'd seen before, and those he'd rewind endlessly.

The Special Needs Child had a daunting list of *couldn'ts*: he couldn't tie his shoes, select and put on his own clothes in the morning, master the use of toilet paper, sleep without getting up and dashing back and forth through the house and yelling for a hour or two in the middle of the night. He couldn't be relied upon to walk into an unfamiliar house or museum or amusement park, even after we'd driven hours to get there, so that a regular feature of our family life was Ellen and I dealing—often badly—with Walker's resistance and Davy's convulsive frustration with the whole mess. Most alarmingly, Walker couldn't tell his parents about his feelings—even feeling ill—so that if he hated or feared something or had a headache, he had to face it alone.

Most telling to the world at large, the Special Needs Child announced his presence in his movements: hopping up and down in place when not skip-running; tilting his head up and having an unaccountable plugged-into-an-electric-outlet look in his eyes; avoiding the gaze of someone speaking to him; keeping at least one index finger in an ear most of the time; and the arms—bent at the elbow, pointing up and out, always moving, moving, moving.

But Ellen and I could—almost every day, even in the face of some of his weirdest behavior—see hints of the Regular Kid peeping through the Special Needs shield. Sometimes the hints were brief and indescribable but definite, like not-quite-subliminal messages on film.

"I don't know why," Ellen might say in our late-night summit over chips and dip and TV, "but Walker seemed very connected today. There was a look in his eye I just can't describe. He seemed clear-headed, you know, observant."

"Yeah," I'd say. "I noticed the same thing." And then we'd be off, trying to pin the feeling down: describing the way he looked at me in the bathtub, a glance he gave Ellen in the car, his intense posture while paging through a book.

Other times the hints were all the more frustrating for being much more definite—he could present both selves in quick succession. One evening at dinner Ellen said, "Davy, would you like more juice?"

Davy said, in the lowest, Big Bopper-ish way he could, "Ooh, baby, that's what I like."

We all burst out laughing. A big grin instantly appeared on Walker's face and a sly, knowing look came into his eyes. He leaned back in his chair, tilting it slightly, and looked at each of us. With his square shoulders, his dark eyebrows, his thick curly brown hair, his muscular body—the nonstop jumping, skipping, running and arm-waving gave him, at age seven, the calves and pecs and glutes of Mighty Mouse—Walker was the picture of a cool older brother.

But this vision was shattered the next moment when he tilted the chair forward again, plunged his fingers into his spaghetti, stuffed a great gob of sauce and noodles into his open mouth, dropped some of the noodles on the floor and smeared his face with spaghetti sauce in the process.

BIRTHDAYS WERE BAD. Birthdays amplified the normally still, stifled voice of panic into emotional Sensurround. And for no special reason, this birthday, his eighth, had been worse for Ellen and me than the others. Slumped together on the couch at midnight after the party, we avoided diving into any post-mortem of the celebration for fear of letting the panic completely take over.

Our guests had been John and Christy, Walker's first Sunday school teachers, and their daughter Heather, a smart, beautiful girl the same age as Walker. John and Christy had been perfect teachers. Open-minded and open-hearted, they had always seen through the Special Needs Child to the Regular Kid underneath. They never looked at Walker through the filter of the autism label, and we loved them for that.

Walker loved them too and beamed when the three of them came into the house. He was happy, thrilled even, but kept his normal boy hidden extremely well. He refused to open any presents. He stuffed chocolate birthday cake into his mouth with his hands. He said nothing. Heather had to act more like a friendly teacher's assistant in her bearing toward Walker than another kid his age. How *should* a young lady respond to a fellow who doesn't speak to her, has icing all over his face, and who won't open her birthday gift?

John and Christy were great, professing to spot progress in Walker's development in spite of his strangeness, and we all had fun. But for Ellen and me, alarms were going off. He was now eight, not in school, and not moving ahead the way we'd expected. He seemed to be backing away from books and reading, wasn't stepping up his social skills, wasn't connecting the verbal abilities he did have—singing and spelling—to actual talking. And he still, *still* didn't say "yes" and "no."

It was midnight, our friends were gone, the boys were finally asleep, and we were staring at the floor, sipping champagne, and vibrating with anxiety. Ellen said, suddenly, "Let's watch that first videotape of Walker. That's always good for us."

It was true. We'd watched it several times in the last few years just for its cheering-up powers. Because we didn't own a video camera and had to borrow one from friends, we only had a few home videos. But the ones we had were precious.

So we put the cassette into the VCR and watched. There he is, a happy, smiling, chubby three-year-old boy facing the camera and jumping up and down in the middle of the sidewalk in front of our house. It is a sunny spring day. No parents are visible on the tape, but they can be heard, all right—loud and clear. Both father and mother are saying, over and over, and often at the same time, "Catch the ball, Walker!"and "Throw the ball back, Walker!" and "Good boy, Walker!" A big red and yellow beach ball flies out from behind the camera. Walker catches it, and then dutifully throws it back.

"What's that?" Ellen suddenly said, suddenly leaning forward and staring at the TV screen. "Rewind the tape. Walker's saying something."

"What? I didn't notice anything," I said, but as the Commander of the Remote Control, I obliged her.

Walker is jumping again, and Ellen and I are talking loudly again, as though we think he is slightly deaf and has to have every word repeated distinctly. Sure enough, Walker is saying something, but I can't make it out. Ellen looks at me and says, "Rewind it again. I can't believe this."

This time through I do understand him and I am astonished and mortified. He's saying, very plainly now, "Look at me!" and "I love you!" but loud voices are so busy with their video camera trying to get the boy to perform the way they expect him to that they don't even notice. In fact, until this viewing (the fourth? the fifth?) five years later, we had never noticed him speaking, so caught up had we been in our preoccupied worrying.

So there he was, a "nonspeaking" boy who was actually speaking to us but we weren't noticing. He wasn't saying anything we wanted him to say or were trying to get him to say, so as far as we were concerned he couldn't really be telling us anything. He was just making noise.

And the awful thought hit us both at the same time: How often has this happened? How often have we, because of the buzzing in our heads, missed what he was actually saying to us? And we were his biggest boosters! We were the ones who, as far as doctors and evaluators were concerned, were hallucinating about his spectacular-but-invisible abilities. And if we, the goofball wishful-thinking parents, could miss something this obvious and basic and flat-out wonderful, how much more would others miss?

So we developed a rule, one that proved both true and painfully hard to live up to: *Walker is always communicating more than even we—his ever-watchful parents—can comprehend.*

In other words, try not to shout at the Special Needs Child when the Regular Kid is standing in front of you.

FOR THE PREVIOUS year Walker had been seeing a new speech therapist, one who at first seemed to work out well. True, she exuded more than a whiff of superiority, but we chalked that up to the fact she was younger than we were and probably felt a need to establish some authority. Walker did seem to like her and she didn't register any strong objections to the fact that we were homeschooling him. We sensed that she didn't approve of our renegade project, and she never, ever said anything encouraging about it, but she didn't hassle us about it either. Considering how anarchic most educators considered the idea (most, we knew, would regard avoidance of special education as the behavior of crazed survivalists or moonshiners in the Ozarks), we felt that she was the best we could do.

She worked in the speech department of yet another well-regarded North Side hospital, so she was our connection to educational respectability. Hers was a name I could blurt out to the cadre of police and truant officers that would doubtless show up at our door some dark and stormy night. "Why yes, as a matter of fact my son does have a *real* teacher," I would say smugly, pulling out a business card, "and here's her telephone number. Why don't you give her a call right now, officer?"

Nevertheless, she grated on our nerves. We began referring to her as Miss Appropriate. She was tall and ladylike and wore appropriate earrings and appropriate dresses and stockings and had perfectly appropriate hair and makeup. It seemed to us that, professionally speaking, she came across as more appropriate for real estate tax law or public relations work than for speech therapy with our wild boy, but that seemed just a quibble.

She always greeted us correctly, with a formal smile and a formal greeting as in, "Good morning, Mr. and Mrs. Hughes. Good morning, Walker. And how are you today?" She studded her conversation with the word "appropriate," as in "Walker tried to kiss me today, but I explained to him that that isn't appropriate." She always called Ellen and me "Mr. and Mrs. Hughes," since, apparently, use of the parents' first names would have mortally gutted her authority. Overall, she managed to convey the impression of stepping down from a great height to make brief professional contact with us.

She believed that children develop in standard, rigid ways, so that when Ellen or I described to her some of the remarkable appearances of the Regular Kid, she showed no interest, as though we'd been telling her about some hallucinations we'd been having. I kept telling her, for instance, about how Walker read, that he'd read some books aloud to us, that he loved reading. One day she caved to my suggestion and presented a book to him. After the lesson she reported that Walker couldn't read, and she'd known beforehand that he couldn't: after all, children need to read single words consistently before they read whole sentences.

Walker had twice-weekly half hour sessions with her, and she seldom failed to say something that would irritate me when she came out to greet him or said good-bye. One morning when she was late she saw him watching the TV in the waiting room. "Hello, Walker! Oh, you like TV?" she said. "Yes, it has such pretty colors doesn't it? You like the colors, don't you? And look how they move!"

My God! I thought. Colors! Is that all she thinks he's capable of getting out of watching TV? After all we've said to her about his reading and how he watches his favorite videos? It was as though she thought of him as a different species—like a fly or a mosquito—that sees things in a totally incomprehensible way.

On another day, after a session so boisterous that he twice ran out of her small office and down the hall, she observed, sagely: "Walker seemed very agitated today. I think he may be upset about the possibility of a war in the Middle East. You might change the channel when the news starts discussing that. Children seem to be very worried that the world might end."

Right, I thought, all those colors moving and changing shape and bumping into each other until—*boom*—world-wide color panic!

It seemed to us that Miss Appropriate could never get past her vision of the Special Needs Child that she assumed Walker to be, could never see him as a distinct person that she could empathize with, could befriend.

Our patience with her began to crack when she began arriving late and ending her sessions with Walker early, trimming ten minutes off a half hour lesson. We had some limited sympathy with this; it was unnerving to try to get Walker to sit still and do some one thing for any length of time. And, like us, she probably felt her efforts weren't getting anywhere, eliciting any measurable improvement. But she seemed increasingly annoyed with Walker, almost to dislike him, and we began to think we'd better cast around for a new teacher.

IT WAS A cold winter morning as I sat trying to ignore Joan Lunden in the waiting room of the speech clinic. I'd been awake most of the night with Walker and I'd done about as badly with him as a parent could, yelling at him and threatening him, ignoring him and joking with him, trying everything I could to put a stop to the uproar. I'd been panicked that the tenant below would move out, for Walker had figured out a way to ratchet up the decibels for his night-time performance: he'd jump up and down on the hardwood floor in the dining room directly over the bedroom where the tenant slept, laughing and looking, successfully, for the hysterical parent reaction.

Ellen and I felt like students in some satanic sleep-deprivation experiment, so little sleep had we had—about three hours a night for the previous month. But unlike subjects in an experiment, there was to be no paycheck and no end in sight.

So I wasn't in the mood to listen to Joan Lunden's chipper advice about child rearing. Joan appeared every morning on the large TV facing the couch where the parents had to sit. This television had no knobs, no volume or channel controls, not even a plug. It just automatically came on with a loud *thunk* at precisely nine a.m. each morning and robotic Joan Lunden came on with it. It was a cable show (or maybe an endless loop of videotape?) that played, loudly and relentlessly and uncontrollably, like some sort of thought control device in a science fiction novel.

Joan was talking, as she always did, about the other world, the world of "normal" parent problems—what to do about ear infections, how to deal with the "terrible two's"—and it wasn't going down well with me at all. Where was Joan last night when I needed her? Ellen and I could have used an Ideal Mom to step in and handle the situation right so we could get a decent five hours of sleep.

I was deep into my Joan Lunden reverie when Miss Appropriate emerged, shocked, from her office, tugging Walker by the hand. Walker had just bitten her (no skin broken) and only a homeschooled autistic child, she said, would do such a thing.

"Oh, I'm sorry," I said. (Apologizing to everybody, even paid professionals, for his behavior had become a reflex.) "He must be very frustrated. It's what he does when he's trying to tell you something." I spoke cheerily, trying to mollify her. It was hard to talk, though, because during this exchange Walker was shouting words I couldn't understand, grabbing at my mouth and clutching my coat and jumping up and down. He clearly had his own version of the biting story, though his speech teacher wasn't catching on.

"What are you trying to say, honey?" I asked him.

She would have none of this.

"He needs structure," she loudly declared. "He needs discipline! He needs to be in Special Ed!"

Unable to talk and handle Walker at the same time, I thought it best just to nod and get out of there as fast as I could. It was a cold, sunny day, and Walker's mood changed as soon as we got into the car. We drove to a Dunkin' Donuts and gorged ourselves for a while. I was wide awake now, and steaming with anger. Why couldn't she see the same boy we did? Why did she persist in seeing in him what she thought she was supposed to see?

Miss Appropriate clearly thought Ellen and I were crazy. We decided that though we didn't want to give up on another speech therapist, we couldn't send Walker back to her, especially in light of the fact that he was making no clear progress with her.

We seemed to be inching even further away from Formal Education and toward…well, what, exactly? We had no answer. But we still believed the free-floating project we had going held the most promise for more frequent sightings of Regular Kid.

NINE

"Nothing is Written"

Ellen and I have some debate over the causes of the tumult of Walker's "first grade," but we're clear on what was responsible for the I-20 incident: parent stupidity.

It was Friday evening a week before Christmas of 1993, and the four of us were stuffed in the Escort going 70 m.p.h. on Interstate 20 (I-20) through the darkness of southern Illinois with the usual load of electronic gadgets, magazines, Coke cans, crackers, hand-held games, maps, and candy wrappers piled around us like postal packing material. We had already been through several of the stages of the yearly ten-hour trip to Grandma's house: expectation of going to see her and twenty or so relatives that descended on her, elation at starting the trip, and weariness at the endless parade of silos, state rest areas, and semi-trucks rocking our little car in their wake. We were now in the stage of denial: pretending to enjoy ourselves, pretending to think we weren't two hours from Grandma's ranch in Tennessee.

Ellen and I had a division of labor on these long trips. I drove. Ellen managed snacks, sandwiches, interesting topics of conversation, spills, the map (I didn't think I should be expected to drive and actually know where I was going at the same time), the boom box in her lap (the car had no tape player), my comfort, and eruptions in the back seat.

Walker, surprisingly enough, usually did pretty well in the car. He'd shout and demand to stop at every rest area, and he'd have to listen to his Raffi tapes over and over (Raffi is a perfectly nice children's singer, I'm sure, but I have learned to hate, with a pure, white-hot hatred, not only him, but his voice, his guitar, his band, his love of nature, his beard, and his chipper attitude), but when I glanced into the back seat, Walker usually had a pleased, even peaceful smile on his face. Davy kept up a steady stream of stories and funny observations, and Ellen and I had a chance for long chats with the boys locked into position behind us. So these trips were generally a pleasant change in our routine.

But not always.

My fantasy was that once in a while during the ten hours to Grandma's we could all listen to a couple of my tapes of 1940s-era Jack Benny shows. I discovered that while Jack's old TV show has not held up over time, the radio programs have. And his series of Christmas programs set in a department store with Mel Blanc as the tormented sales clerk are just wonderful. My insistence on this kind of fogeyish stuff—Ellen calls it "Bob's Little World"—was tolerated pretty well by my little tribe, but they had limits.

"Listen to this. It's just great," I said as we sped down the highway through the darkness.

"POOP!" Walker yelled.

"It's not too far to the next rest area," Ellen said. "Just a little bit further, Walker."

"POOP! POOOOOP!"

"Jack has just changed his mind again about buying the plastic-tipped shoelaces," I went on, determinedly cheery. "Listen to how Mel Blanc reacts."

"Shut up, Walker!" Davy commanded. "Do we have to listen to Jack Benny? All the time, Jack Benny, Jack Benny, Jack Benny."

"Shush, Davy. Believe me. You'll like this part."

Just then there was a strange roaring-whooshing-humming noise.

"Walker opened his door!" Davy shrieked.

I turned in the darkness and there he was, his seatbelt unbuckled, his door open several inches. Both Ellen and I started screaming, "CLOSE THE DOOR, WALKER! CLOSE THE DOOR!" while I kept one hand on the steering wheel and the other clutching his arm. Ellen, completely twisted around in her seat, managed to grab the door handle and pull it shut.

Ellen spent the rest of the trip facing Walker from the front seat and holding down his door lock. We were all silent after that: Ellen and I anxious and shaken, Davy no doubt wishing he could be airlifted into another family.

Why did Walker do it? Did he hate the claustrophobia and tedium of the ride, and so—unable to express himself—pulled the most dramatic stunt he could think of? Did he think he could make a restroom appear by just willing it? Was he nervous about going to Tennessee and seeing all his relatives? Was he curious about how we'd react if he did the unthinkable? Did he want to see what driving was like with a door open? Was it a joke? Or did he just think anything, even tumbling out of a speeding car, was better than hearing Jack Benny one more time?

Who knew? Who cared?

Ellen and I were frozen with only one question: Could we keep him safe?

This was answered for us a few weeks later with a hesitant "possibly." A friend pointed out to me that even our cheap tiny Escort had a child lock on the door for the very emergency we had faced. So, my friend was kind enough not to point out, if we had read our owner's manual—or knew what apparently everyone else in the world knew about their cars—the whole brainless near-catastrophe wouldn't have occurred.

Besides our total automotive ignorance, the incident brought home to us the sheer fright of not knowing what Walker would or wouldn't do in any given situation. Talking helps a parent understand the child and limn the boundaries of what the child is capable of: Jason is nutty enough that he just might jump out a window; Jennifer is sensible and wouldn't dream of it. But with silent Walker the mere fact that he hadn't done something dangerous before was no help in feeling assured that he would never actually do it. In this sense Walker, at eight, was still a toddler.

At eight a. m. two days into the visit things were not going well, not going well at all.

Walker was screaming and leaping up and down on the bed in the bedroom the four of us always slept in, throwing himself around the room and picking up lamps, sheets, anything he could get his hands on to pitch at the walls or at anybody who tried to stop him. I was in the shower in the bathroom nearby and could hear him, so I was hurrying as fast as I could to get out and help with him.

As I leaned over to pick up a towel, I suddenly felt a sensation in my lower back as though a Samurai warrior had been hiding behind the shower curtain and, just when my back was turned, plunged his sword up through my spinal column. In an instant, I could see with perfect clarity the next hour or two or six or ten and the stress I was about to pile onto the whole tense situation. I tried to straighten up, but the pain pitched me into Hunchback of Notre Dame posture. Painfully pulling on some clothes, I painfully stepped into the bedroom and saw Walker bouncing up from the mattress so high his head touched the ceiling as Ellen tried to restrain him. He had already bitten her hands several times, and she wondered if he had actually broken the bed.

"Maybe I can drive him around again. Maybe that will help settle him down," I said, heroically I thought, through gritted teeth.

"Oh, no, not your back again! What's next?" Ellen shouted above the screaming. "Driving around won't do it. He wants to go home."

"Yeah, I can see that," I said as he lunged at me, mouth open, and my sister Pat, who had been helping Ellen, tried to peel him off me.

My five brothers and sisters had all, one after another, taken a hand in trying to help, but everybody was clueless. Walker was on a serious tear, and sternness, physical restraint, humor—nothing could stop him. It looked to everybody like one of those unaccountable, psychotic things autistic kids do, but Ellen and I knew the cause.

This trip and these people meant the world to him. Night after night starting weeks before the trip, Walker, Davy and I had sat on the couch and read our *Over the River and Through the Woods* book just before bedtime. Each night when we got to the end, Walker always shouted the last line, "Hurrah for the pumpkin pie!" His constant refrain all through the month of November was "Grandma Ruth! Grandma Ruth!"

And his expectations each year had always paid off. Grandma Ruth and Grandpa Jack had a big, sprawling ranch house with horses and cows and 150 acres of rolling hills. The woodsmoke in the air, the pine trees, the deer, the brown hills, the red sunsets—all were refreshing for me and my three brothers and two sisters and their families, since none of this was part of our Chicago-suburbs-and-city background. Our father died in 1968 and my mother remarried Jack, a big-hearted telephone executive who had a dream: to start a new career after retirement by building a ranch house and raising cattle.

Walker took to Grandpa Jack's dream place like it was Disney World. In previous years he'd ride the pony Jack had expressly bought for the grandchildren. He'd run around the enormous yard with the abandon of a kid who never got to run freely. And most important of all, he'd see his adored grandmother and grandfather, aunts, uncles, and cousins, people he got to see only once or twice a year. It was in front of them that he got to show off his little skills. In previous years he had played a rudimentary form of living room soccer with his cousin Eric. He had read a short children's book—aloud, with feeling—to a big, cheering crowd of family. He had sat on his Uncle Larry's lap and been tickled, played catch with his Uncle Pete, rolled in piles of leaves with his cousins.

But this trip was different. For one thing, it rained every minute we were there, so outdoor activities halted, turning the house into an emotional pressure cooker for him. For another, he was too old for all his brilliant-but-silent toddler stuff and hadn't visibly moved beyond it, so he had been forced to confront his own inability to communicate with his relatives. He had watched Davy, his little brother, come on strong. Davy could talk to everyone, play with everyone, pull everybody's eyes toward himself.

And I hadn't been the friend, ally, and interpreter I usually was. I was worried that I wouldn't get through the book I had assigned for the extra class I taught at Northwestern's University College. Every chance I got I hunkered down in a quiet room and tried to plow through that week's assignment, half of Dickens' *Bleak House*. I'd turned myself into a sort of tension radiator, and Walker, sensitive to every nuance in the emotional atmosphere, had absorbed all my stress.

For the first time Walker sensed the invisible but real fence between him and everyone there. He paced back and forth in the hallway—which was the front entrance of the house, connected the kitchen and bedrooms, and opened wide on the living room—where he was sure to see or jostle everyone coming and going through the house. He held his arms up, bent at the elbow, and waved his hands in the air. He walked on tiptoe, forwards, then backwards, wearing a groove through the floor, looking at the ceiling or out the window going "Ah, ah, ah ah!" as if he could see some astonishing sight invisible to everyone but him. His Uncle Ron, who had easy rapport with children, would walk by and say, "Hey, how's it going, Walker?" Walker would look through him, seeming not to care, and Uncle Ron, at a loss about how to connect with him, would pass by. This sort of thing happened over and over, each family member saying something to Walker from time to time and Walker smiling, making eye contact or looking away, but never responding with anything anyone could grab and run with.

Walker did this strange hallway dance for two days and watched. He watched us play a game of charades from this spot, watched his cousins happily pound on the synthesizer-organ, watched us watch TV. He never went off by himself but stayed always in everybody's way, unavoidable, always insisting, without speaking the actual words, "Here I am! Look at me!"

Ellen and I knew that Walker, far from being lost in an "autistic" world of his own, was right there, at that moment, in a devastatingly acute way. He would have liked to gobble everybody up: talk to them, touch them, impress them, sing songs, knock their socks off with friendliness, but he knew he couldn't do it. His beloved Aunt Pat, who used to have a special, hugging-and-kidding relationship with him, would like to play with him now but doesn't know how.

So there he was, on the third day of our stay, pulling the house to pieces. Ellen looked from her son to her husband—from the Tazmanian Devil, pinned to the floor by Aunt Pat, to Quasimodo, wincing in pain—and made an executive decision.

"We're getting out of here. Now."

Of course, this left Davy broken-hearted. His expectations for the Thanksgiving trip were as stratospherically high as Walker's.

How many of these aborted fun occasions will Davy remember as an adult? Will he rattle them off in a horrific litany to a psychiatrist? Will he write them all up as a "Daddy and Mommy Dearest" book?

ON THE INTERSTATE about a hundred miles south of Chicago and about 400 miles from the ranch, it was dark, icy rain was thrashing our tiny space capsule of a car, and the traffic was insanely fast. I was driving because, with the samurai sword in my back, it was the simplest job for me to be doing. Ellen was exhausted and twisted around in her seat with her eye on Walker behind her (he had calmed down as soon as he realized we were headed home) to make sure he didn't jump out of the car, and she was trying, ineffectually, to boost Davy's spirits. So we pulled off into a Holiday Inn with an indoor pool, always a popular decision with the boys.

When Ellen had carried all the clothes and junk from the car and settled us all in, we noticed Walker start to do something strange. He was over near the door and said, "Cinderella! Cinderella!" He looked upwards and gestured with his raised arm. He then walked back and forth in the narrow Holiday Inn space between the beds and the TV, saying sentences in a dramatic, modulated voice, but we could only make out a few of the words: "Lucifer," "Fairy Godmother," "ball." It dawned on us that he was actually re-enacting a scene from the Disney "Cinderella," and he seemed to be reciting it word-for-word.

Ellen, Davy, and I sat on the beds and watched the show, straining to make out what he was saying. He walked in front of us, reciting, peeking at us from time to time to see our reaction. His cheeks were pinker than usual, his eyes shone more than usual, and he walked on tiptoe. He would stop, say something, rush to the corners of the room, stop again. After a while he paused, turned his back to us, and seemed to be thinking. Then we heard him say to himself, in a casual voice quite different from his stage voice, "Let's see now. How does it go?" He turned around as though he was dancing with a partner, holding his arm around her, or him—he seemed to be Cinderella through most of the performance—and sang "So This is Love," the song that Cinderella sang while dancing at the ball.

When he was through with the performance we all three applauded him and cheered. Ellen and I then went through the usual motions of motel "fun" with the boys in the steamy, crowded pool, and the motel "fun" of getting tired, overstimulated boys to sleep, all the time in a state of euphoric astonishment, all the time wondering, What else is he hiding?

Later, with the TV off and boys asleep, Ellen and I had our conference.

I whispered in the darkness, "So. What's the deal with that? *Let's see now. How does it go?*' How can he say that? He's never said anything like that before. This, after his boy-from-space routine yesterday. How can he turn it on and turn it off?"

"It's like he's trying to show us what he can do because he felt too tense at the ranch," Ellen whispered. "I think he felt like such a failure in front of his relatives that he wanted to prove something to us, like he's trying to re-humanize himself."

"If he can have a weird blip of clarity like this, why can't he have more of them?" I said.

"Can you believe it? Cinderella!" Ellen said, or something a lot like it, for after chattering on like this for a while we both passed out, relieved and unspeakably happy.

THIS SPARKLING LITTLE Broadway moment in the motel—revealing Walker's submerged sense of poetry and romance, love of stories, as well as his verbal ability—turned out to be just that, an isolated moment. In the ensuing few months nothing so showy and definite occurred to reassure us, but much happened that dampened our hopes.

HIS SLEEPING PROBLEMS continued. Since birth, he'd go through periods of, at his very best, only a few weeks without waking up in the middle of the night. Most of the time he'd get up at 1 or 2 or 3 a.m. and start jumping on his bed and yelling; one of us would leap up, run downstairs and get him out of the room so Davy could sleep and the downstairs tenant wouldn't be disturbed. Walker would stay up for one, sometimes two or more hours yelling, running around the house, grabbing us and trying to bite us, jumping up and down on the floor, and worst of all, laughing.

Walker, age 9, in his diningroom/bedroom

The laughter was the killer. We knew that children occasionally woke up from nightmares and cried in fright and needed parents to comfort them, but his loud, uncontrolled laughter was maddening. Though we'd try to spell each other, taking turns getting up with him on alternate nights, there was no relief. Since our "mezzanine" bedroom shared the same airspace as the living room where the drama played out each night, neither of us actually slept.

We tried stratagems that usually centered around trying to ignore him. We'd pull out the dining room table and make a sleeping area for him with a pillow and sleeping bag. Then we'd watch TV or read or pretend to sleep on the couch. We'd turn all the lights on or turn them all off. But he always had our number. His supersensitive emotional barometer registered the true emotional pressure in the air, no matter how hard we tried to mask it. We'd give off anger or frustration or anxiety or exhaustion, sometimes all at the same time, and he'd react.

One snowy night in March of 1994, about 2 a.m., I was at a loss about what to do. His midnight self was in full battle gear, and ignoring him was not an option. For an hour and a half, he'd been shouting, laughing, and running back and forth through the house. He'd discovered a new trick: running several steps up the stairs, turning around, and leaping down to the floor, slamming it as hard as he could with his feet. The house would shake, the dishes would rattle, and we'd try not to think about what it sounded like downstairs.

About the third time he did this, I grabbed him by the shoulders and he lunged at me, mouth open, and tried to bite me. We became welded together like two wrestlers with no idea how to fight.

"Stop it now, Walker! It's the middle of the night. You need to be sleeping!"

"How are you doing? Do you need help?" Ellen called from upstairs.

"No, there's nothing you can do! Get off, Walker! Get off me now!" I was peeling his arm off my neck with my right hand and with my left pushing his mouth away from my face. When I had disengaged his left arm, I hit him on his shoulder with my fist until he let go of my neck from the other side. When he started to laugh, I hit him on the shoulder a couple more times just for the hell of it.

"Lie down! Right here right now!" I yelled, pointing at the sleeping bag, while he flinched away from me and kneaded his shoulder in pain. "I have to sleep, Walker. You have to sleep so I can get some sleep! Lie down and close your eyes! God damn you, Walker!"

With these words of reassurance and encouragement to my scared, mentally disabled son, I turned away, stomped over to the couch, and turned on the TV set. I sat shaking and wondering about my anger while he lay awake for only a short time longer and fell asleep.

It was one of those middle of the night moments when it seemed to me that anybody pulled off the street at random—even in our neighborhood—could do a better job of fathering than I.

Miserable, guilt-ridden, and despairing about him, I was way too wound up to do any sleeping. So I surfed the TV channels until my pulse was normal and my head was no longer buzzing, and stopped when I hit "Lawrence of Arabia." I adored this movie when it came out in the early sixties. I remembered seeing it on a sub-zero weekend night in January when I was stressed out from high school. I was a freshman at a boys' Catholic school on the South Side of Chicago and my life was a dark tunnel of work, tests, and competition over grades. This film swept me into a different world. The music, the desert, the adventure, and the "adult" portrayal of the hero took me somewhere far away and distracting and exhilarating.

This night, as I watched Lawrence—the city slicker, the greenhorn, the naive Englishman—interminably cross the desert with a few dozen Arabs, I wondered how such a slow-moving film had once meant so much to me. I thought to myself: This will put me to sleep very nicely.

Lawrence, unrealistically gorgeous and appealingly neurotic, is played by Peter O'Toole; the leader of the Arabs is played by the even more unrealistically good-looking Omar Sharif. After getting across the brutal, huge, soporific expanse of sand, they discover that one Arab is missing—he must have fainted and fallen off his camel somewhere back in the vastness of the desert. O'Toole, our hero, says they must go back and get him. But the Arabs, with centuries of frequent-camel-miles experience, treat him like a silly, effete British tourist. The lost man is dead, one of them says.

"No one can cross the desert and live," a wise-sounding Arab says. "It is written."

But our hero mounts his camel and says angrily, "Nothing is written" and starts back over the intolerable distance. At this point I started to get interested in spite of myself, and the swelling music and sandstorms started to become fascinating. After a minute I was on the edge of my chair and rooting for Lawrence as he looks for the man in a wilderness that has no signposts, no life.

When he returns with the man, who is still alive and slung over the back of his camel, the Arabs greet Lawrence with utter astonishment and cheers. The exhausted, sand-blasted hero looks down from his camel perch at Omar Sharif and says in a clipped, Peter O'Toolish way, ladling scorn into every syllable, "Nothing is written!"

I nearly leaped up from the chair. "That's it!" I said out loud. "'Nothing is written!'"

I thought: Of course it's chump behavior to keep hoping for Walker when all the experts tell us he's lost. Of course things look very, very bad for him. But in a real way *nothing has been written* that fully makes sense to us, that seems to take in our boy in all his mysterious atypical-ness. There is no agreed-upon cause of autism, no spot in Walker's brain that shows up on a test that doctors could point to and say, "Aha, there it is. There's the autism, by jiminy." And most telling of all, there was nothing written for the anguished, despairing parent coping with the impossible in the middle of the night. Some few autistics get well, write books, have children, and no one can explain why.

Why not Walker?

Unlike the lost Arab, Walker was right there right at that moment, in front of me, impossible to ignore. He was begging not to be left behind, demanding help every minute of the day and night, yearning like Cinderella for a piece of the wide world he was locked out of.

I decided to tuck away this little scene in my mind and take Lawrence's words as my mantra. I resolved to repeat his line to myself—"Nothing is written, Bob"—when crowds gather around a screaming Walker and stare and shake their heads, when doctors and therapists predict doom for him, when my own despair about him rears its ugly head. I would try to adopt Peter O'Toole's scorn and hauteur in the face of conventional wisdom and remember that I'm free to adopt any attitude I choose.

So it was absurd to do this. So what? Who cares? It would be my own little secret.

TEN

Maureen

It wasn't going to be easy to sit atop the camel of independence and lope across the desert of child development with nerve and a true heart when everybody was telling us to give up on Walker and grieve and maybe, just maybe—if we handed him over to the developmental police officers in time—he'd learn to…tie his shoes.

We knew we couldn't do it alone and had to find good teachers who were open-minded enough to believe in his possibilities. Tired of feeling like anarchist crazies in denial, we wanted allies with credentials—at least one "expert" who saw what we saw in him: the boy we saw just behind the film of autism.

So Ellen, the family ambassador to the real world and its true explorer, set out to do some reconnaissance. The result was that a well-regarded autism specialist from a well-regarded program run by a local state university was scheduled to come over to the house and give us some advice.

Early one hot spring evening we heard heavy, irregular footfalls on the front steps, so we peeked through the ever-droning fan in the window. A hefty young woman was slowly making her ascent, huffing and puffing and pausing for breath. Walker, the hypersensitive emotion barometer of the family, seemed to sense what was coming,

ran into the back porch room of the house and shut the door. Davy
went upstairs to play his Nintendo game and try to shut out the inter-
minable discussion of his brother's problems.

After she'd planted herself on our shaky couch and gulped a glass
of ice water, she asked us to tell Walker's story, beginning with his
birth.

Ellen and I launched into what we had come to call The Speech,
our tag-team narrative of Walker's story that we had already rattled off
so often to doctors and therapists and friends that it seemed like some
kind of long-running Broadway show. We hated having to deliver The
Speech; it meant going over and over the same territory with yet
another disbelieving person. But like old troupers, whenever we got
going with it, we started to get ardent about it. The Speech always
began with a description of Walker's normal birth and our insistence
in the face of much skepticism—"Are you *sure?*... How was his Apgar
score?... You say he never shrank away from being held or touched?"
—that there were no signs of his coming troubles until just before the
age of two.

Listening to The Speech must have been a weird experience for
anyone committed to the dogma of autism-as-unqualified-disaster.
Our strangeness revealed itself in our enthusiasm as we warmed to the
subject: our admiration of Walker's spirit, intelligence and abilities; our
insistence on the significance of small details of his behavior; our
spooky unanimity of opinion (we only disagreed to insist that the
other's statement was even more true than it seemed). The listener was
usually looking for signs of conflict, cracks in the story indicating
trouble in the marriage and dysfunction in the family. Ellen and I had
found that no matter how loud was the overt insistence on the principle that *The parents are not to blame*, the expert usually managed to send
off more than a whiff of the idea that *Well of course the kid's
autistic—look at the two of you!*

Irritatingly enough, we'd plow ahead as though we were one
speaker, not two. We knew our story well, for we had honed it many
nights over chips and salsa and Letterman, perfecting the patter,
adding to the story and tinkering with its parts in the light of new

developments. It was our big project after all: working with Walker, staring at him, interpreting him, keeping his hopes and ours alive.

So the autism expert of the moment was left with nothing to note except that Ellen and I were equally nuts, equally possessed by the same illusion that we could see our son without peering through the lens of the expert, without adopting the jargon and accepting the orthodoxy of hopelessness.

To a skeptic, the most bizarre aspect of our story was the fact that anything Walker did, no matter how dark and weird, was given a positive—often *desperately* positive—spin. At age four, we'd say, he started biting the dining room table and screaming. The big cheap pine table eventually had permanent tiny teeth marks like miniature piano keys around its whole perimeter. Our take on this? *Obviously, doing something with his mouth meant he was trying to speak to us but was blocked for some strange reason.* At age six he went through a three-month period of pulling his pants down and defecating in the corner of our bedroom. We'd be downstairs in the living room and suddenly we'd sense *something different in the air,* but What was it? Ah, we'd realize a moment later: He's done it again. Our interpretation: *A bizarre, even despairing, experiment to break through the horrible prison he found himself in. It was a way to get something, anything out, in any way he could, to break through the barrier. It was so much better than his silence. It showed us he wasn't satisfied with his situation.*

"We were almost happy," Ellen would say, "when he started to poop in our bedroom."

"Yes," I'd say, picking up on the theme, "the pooping was clearly a step forward. Disturbing…but very exciting too."

WHEN WE GOT to the poop portion of the Walker biography on this particular steamy evening in May, I could see that our expert was growing impatient and starting to tune us out. She nodded and waved a magazine-fan at her face. She squinted and smiled sadly. She leaned hard on repetition of the "O-Kaaaaayyyyy" that means "Will these people *never* stop talking?"

Interrupting us in mid-spiel, she said: "At our clinic we have classes for parents of autistic children. Would you be interested in coming?"

"Really?" said Ellen, still in enthusiastic mode. "Would you like us to guest lecture about our experiences and, well, share some of what we've learned?"

"Not exactly. I was thinking more in terms of you *taking* our classes and understanding autism better. You have a lot to learn and would benefit from listening to other parents. You really need to get Walker into special education. You've lost valuable time by teaching him at home, but perhaps all is not lost."

A torrent of angry incoherence was welling up in my voicebox, and I knew I had to get the hell out of the room. "Excuse me," I said with a smile. "I think I hear Walker in the back. I'd better check up on him."

Ellen had a rule: *Stay friendly. Don't burn any bridges. Win an argument, lose a possible lead. You never know when someone may give you a hint or help make a connection that will prove of use later.*

"I was simply respecting your rule, Honey," I guiltily explained to her later. "There was no way I could go on sitting there without saying something really stupid."

To our visitor, Ellen and I were fiddling while Rome burned. We needed to be *taught* hopelessness—and fast. We needed to wipe the strangely inappropriate grins off our faces. *(The lunacy of these people to be proud of their son when they should be miserable!)* Only then would we become good, sane parents.

Ellen stayed and smiled and chatted and got a name and number of someone else who later offered her another name and number of a speech therapist who was highly recommended and was finishing up her doctorate at Northwestern.

An appointment was made for the therapist to make a house visit.

ON AN OVERCAST day in June of 1993 we were sitting on the couch and waiting. My spirits were at a new low. *Why did this woman insist on coming over to the house?* I was asking myself. *To check out the*

Wacky Homeschoolers in Natural Habitat? To lecture us on how obviously bad our child-rearing choices had been?

The expression on my face must have worried Ellen because she suddenly said, "Take it easy. We've got to keep looking for people who can help us. We can't do this alone. Besides, you never know when you'll find somebody good."

I nodded in fake agreement and let out a sigh at her naiveté as though shaking my head over punctuation errors in student papers.

Then we noticed a young woman lightly coming up our front steps. When the bell rang, Davy dashed to the back room to work on the computer and Walker zoomed up the stairs to our bedroom and disappeared.

I turned the first deadbolt, then the second deadbolt, then the chain, and finally the top deadbolt and opened the door.

"Hi, I'm Maureen Sweeney," she said cheerily.

"Hello, I'm Bob, Walker's dad, and this is Ellen," I said.

Here we go again, I noted to myself.

She sat down on the couch, and we pulled up straight-backed dining room chairs to position ourselves in front of her for the usual delivery of The Speech.

But something was different this time.

In part it was the way she looked. The physical opposite of Miss Appropriate, she wore loose slacks and a loose shirt and running shoes and had shiny black hair cut short. She was good-looking, but not in the real estate sales or investment banking sort of way. She seemed ready for action, for whatever a wild, physical boy might throw at her. And her eyes had an arresting intelligence about them that was hard to define but very real.

In part it was the way she listened. She didn't just hear the words, she heeded them. Her "OK" seemed to indicate hearty agreement: *Yes, we're on the same wavelength.* Her body language—her eyes, her lightly ironic smile—said *I know just what you mean—that's exactly the way it is.*

Thus when we got to the poop chapter of the story and told her our upbeat interpretation of it, Maureen didn't flinch in revulsion. She said:

"Yes, I couldn't agree more. He was trying to communicate with you, certainly."

And when we reached the point in the Speech where smoke alarms started going off in the minds of other teachers and therapists, i.e., the decision to homeschool Walker, she said:

"I think you made a wise choice. I like everything I'm hearing."

At that point Ellen and I looked at each other and smiled: *She doesn't think we're jerks!*

Our adventures with Miss Appropriate brought out something like scorn from Maureen. She told us that a lot of therapists are developmental in their approach and insist a child has to do A before he does B. "Unfortunately, they don't want the parent to have any opinions. They pretty much just do what the textbook from grad school told them to do. I don't have any ideology at all. I take my cues from the child himself. Every kid is different."

"So you wouldn't hammer away at getting Walker to put blocks in a mailbox forever, the way his first speech teacher did?" I asked her, then immediately regretted the question. I felt as though I'd just asked a Chess Grand Master if he would try the gambit of a loser.

She smiled. "I didn't go into the field to babysit. I *know* I can help these children. I expect dramatic change."

Listening to her, I felt a strange sensation of *lift*, as though a huge bar bell had been taken off my shoulders. Ellen looked at me and back at Maureen and smiled and said, "You sound too good to be true." Maybe it was my imagination playing tricks on me, but it seemed as though she *liked* us.

If there were a Disney cartoon video of our saga, this was the scene when the storm clouds would lift, the sun would break through, and the cute animal sidekicks of the hero would start dancing around the forest. Here was somebody, the first professional really, to see Walker as unique and not simply a specimen of autism. Here was somebody bringing the cool breeze of confidence into the house.

Then Maureen looked up toward our bedroom. Our eyes followed hers. Walker was watching and listening from upstairs, his chin on the railing, his fingers in his ears, and his elbows splayed out on either side.

"Hey, Walker," Ellen called up to him. "This is your new speech teacher, Maureen. We've been telling her all about you."

"Hello, Walker. Why don't you come on down? I'd like to meet you," Maureen said.

Hunched over with his fingers in his ears, Walker quickly came down the stairs. I pulled out another straight-backed chair for him to sit in, and Maureen got up and sat next to him in the middle of the living room.

She leaned over and spoke to him quietly and naturally, *as though he could understand the words!* "I know other boys and girls like you, Walker. I've helped them and I know I can help you."

As she talked, Walker sat perfectly still and looked very thoughtful and listened to everything she was saying. Ellen and I had never seen anything like this. We hadn't even expected him to sit down or stay in one spot for her. But there he was, sitting like a proper student, hanging on her words.

It was love.

MAUREEN PROCEEDED, IN twice-a-week sessions at our house, to play hide-and-seek with him, shout and laugh with him, chase him down the hall, roll him up in a rug, and hug him, as she said, "To squeeze the words out." She established trust and friendship before expecting him to sit at a table and do lessons. She was bitten—over and over—had her hair pulled, and was treated to Walker's wildest stuff. She was unfazed. It was as though she had infrared vision that detected the Regular Kid in the darkness or radar that sensed his other self behind the clouds.

The boy we knew was the boy she saw.

Maureen's visits were great for me. They coincided with Davy's swimming lessons, so Walker and I were left home alone. When Maureen arrived, I'd plunge into Bob's Little World, located in the rear porch room. With the door closed, I'd lean back in the swivel chair, put my feet up on the desk, watch squirrels in the oak tree outside the window, and drink strong coffee. I would listen to my Jack Benny radio tapes or a book on tape, or I'd re-read a chapter or two in a novel by Anthony Trollope. I was *off duty*, a very, very rare experience. I could hear happy yelling, running, tumbling, tickling, giggling. They seemed to be chasing each other and having fun, or sometimes they seemed to be having trouble and locking horns, but the key thing was—*it was none of my business.*

This was an extraordinary feeling. Various tutors we had hired would sooner or later demand that Ellen or I sit there during the session to help keep him on task, interpret him, or just keep him from dashing out of the building. They gave us the impression that they had never seen such a difficult child. Walker was so low-functioning, as far they were concerned, that he had dropped clean out of sight and functions other than, say, brushing his teeth or drinking from a straw were unrealistically lofty goals, like asking a chimp to translate Proust.

One day at the end of their session I came out and found them dancing to a bouncy Roy Rogers song Maureen was playing on our stereo:

> "Oh, it looks you were born to lose,
> Well, sometimes it feels that way.
> Oh, but don't give up, tomorrow
> Just might be your lucky day.
>
> It's an up and down world
> And you can't change it.
> Might get a chance to rearrange it.
> If you hold on, partner,
> Good things are comin' to you.
> *Hold on!* "

Maureen's back was turned to me and Walker seemed to be shaking her to pieces, bouncing up and down in her arms, his legs a fulcrum twisted around her waist, and his face transfixed in rapture beaming at me over her shoulder. They both shouted the final "Hold on!" together, and I applauded.

After putting him down and gasping for breath, Maureen said, "Walker did great today. He read three pages to me from this book."

She showed me *Arthur's Teacher Trouble.*

"Wow," I said. "I haven't been able to get him to do much reading at all lately. I can't get him to sit still long enough."

"Did you try sitting on him?"

"Huh?"

"Sitting on him. He laughs a lot, but he reads the words too."

I laughed out of pure joy just looking at the two of them. There they stood, side by side, grinning. Tugging on Maureen's arm was a boy who knew that at least one good thing was coming to him, every Monday and Wednesday at two o'clock.

Maureen and Walker, age 16

ONE OF MAUREEN'S gifts was her sense that Walker's problem was like ordinary "shyness" taken to the hundredth power. Walker was like the teenage boy who starts to dial the phone to ask the girl to the dance, stops in mid-dial, gets his courage up, tries again, puts the phone down again. The big difference was that Walker was capable of seeing every conceivable situation as a scary "beginning," an "intro" in the terminology of Donna Williams. His problem stretched way beyond simply meeting people (which would have been intelligible), but watching a video, getting in the car, sitting down to work with numbers, trying something new to eat, going through the door of a building, kicking a soccer ball. And once his approach–avoidance dance got into full swing, it seemed like it could go on forever. This is one reason Maureen sat on him, squeezed him, chased him: she was trying to power through his astonishing reluctance and fear and get him to loosen up to *do* things.

Ellen and I wished we had an army of Maureens on call through the day and night to help us deal with his "intros," for they had an explosive effect on all of us.

TAKE THE PUTTING on Shoes Before Church Intro. On a Sunday morning, an hour before getting ready for church, I'd start giving sermons to myself about patience and understanding and start internally adopting a Maureen-style overpowering positive attitude. When the time came to start the shoe ritual, I'd cheerily take him over to the couch, cheerily put his socks and shoes on his feet, double-knot the laces, pat him on the leg, and say, cheerily, "There you go man, all ready for church school!" While the rest of us got ourselves together, he'd quietly take his shoes and socks off. So I'd go at it again. Still somewhat good-naturedly, optimistically wearing my sport coat, I'd put the shoes on his feet again. Then he'd tear them off. Adopting a more commanding, give-no-quarter attitude, I would put them on, tripled-knotted. He'd take them off right away. Soon we were late for his Sunday school.

"Let's go, Walker!" Davy would say, "Come on, Walker, just put them on."

And so it would go: on, off, on, off, until Ellen would take a turn and I'd stomp around the house, my coat and tie off, muttering un-churchly expletives.

Then he would inexplicably pull himself together and keep the shoes on, or we'd lose the battle, throw up our hands and stay home, or we'd put him in the car and hope to get his shoes on later, but the wear and tear, especially on Davy, was terrible.

An amateur Walker observer might conclude that he was "voting with his feet" and didn't like church. But we knew his problem was just the opposite. Like the teenager afraid to phone the beautiful girl, Walker found church *too* exciting and wonderful and his failure to get into the swing of it with the other children unbearable. He'd happily shout "CHURCH! CHURCH!" in the car on the way. Or he'd sit quietly with his fingers in his ears, smiling and staring out the window. And he liked it when we talked about his class and his teachers.

Deep in the heart of the intro problem was the paradoxical sense that whatever he was about to do *was just too thrilling to do.*

OR TAKE THE Ice Skating Intro. One Saturday afternoon in February the four of us went to a big indoor rink, rented ice skates and got onto the ice. Then Walker took me completely by surprise. He started doing a fine impression of a normal kid. Though he'd never before been on skates, he stayed up on them, shuffled down the ice at a good clip, and made two circuits around the rink. I skated along beside him, praising him and holding his arm when he seemed about to fall. Listening to the loud music in the rink with hundreds of people skating along in the same direction, I had the sunny sensation that we were just two more happy faces in a happy crowd, doing the normal Saturday father–son thing—we were *having it.*

It was such a great success, and Walker seemed so proud of himself, that I took him back the next week, and the next, and the next. We returned at least a dozen more weekends with this result: *He never once put on the skates again.* He'd get into the car with eagerness, shout "Skating! Skating!" He'd stand in line patiently to rent the skates. Then he'd let me help him put on one of his skates, and while I was fussing with the other one, he'd take the first one off, and so on, and so on. We became such a fixture of the lobby that the woman behind the rental counter took pity on us and handed over the skates free of charge as soon as she saw us coming. Inevitably, I could get him only just inside the door, and he would dash to the corner of the lobby/dressing area farthest from the ice rink itself and start to jump in place, looking almost frightened. Every few minutes he'd sit down on a bench to put on his skates, then take off the skates, get up and jump nervously in place again. If I said, "OK, let's go home now, Walker," he'd sit down fast and try to put on his skates again.

Finally, I couldn't take it any longer, and our skating career bit the dust.

THE GETTING OUT of the Car Intro, in a way, was the worst of all because it meant a one, two, or three-hour car trip was another small catastrophe. Even an aborted short errand could take on cosmic dimensions.

I was standing one lovely spring day on the passenger side of the car holding the door open for Walker. "Come on, come on," I said, "We don't have much time. We'll just run over to the toy store and pick up something. It will only be a minute." Walker moved his leg, put his foot on the ground, then quickly moved his leg back into the car.

We were parallel parked on a shady street in the upscale DePaul area of town and we had to move fast. We were picking up a baby shower gift Ellen had ordered and we were already late.

"Let's go, NOW!" I shout-whispered at him. Then the internal homily began: *Bob, you're losing your temper. Relax, take your time, and firmly but gently encourage him.*

I took a deep breath and looked around. We were parked in front of an elegant old brick two-flat house and a woman who looked like she'd just stepped out of a Smith and Hawken catalog was kneeling and digging in a flower bed. I turned toward the car, put my hand on his shoulder, and said, "OK, Walker. It's time now. Let's go!"

Again, the leg out, the foot on the ground, followed by the swift recoil back into the car. So I took another breath and looked around some more. Two boys about ten years old dressed in Little League uniforms passed on the sidewalk. "See ya!" one of them said to the other, and they split up, one of them approaching the woman on the grass.

"Hi, Mom!" he said.

"How was your game?" she asked him.

"We won."

Then Mrs. Smith and Hawken paused, put down her little spade, and turned to look at her son. "I didn't ask you if you *won*," she said with a stern edge to her voice. "I asked you *how the game was.*"

Somehow, tense as I was about getting Walker out of the car, the sheer irony of the scene hit me hard. Here we were, two adults of about the same age, dressed alike (surely I was "Mr. L.L. Bean"), middle class (though admittedly I was hanging on to the bottom of the category by my fingertips), but we may as well have been The Woman of the Future and Neanderthal Man for all the parenting worlds we had in common. Here was a mother so accustomed to micro-managing her offspring that even friendly conversation morphed into a grim lesson in verbal precision. And here was I, so accustomed to zero control and zero speech that I would have jumped at a deal with the devil for a moment like this:

Walker strolls home from a baseball game with a pal, bids him a friendly good-bye, and saunters over to me as I dig in my garden.

"Hi, Dad," he says.

"How was your game, Son?" I ask with a smile.

"Go to hell, Old Man!"

"Very well, Son!" I say, and whistling a happy tune, go back to my digging.

THOUGH MAUREEN HAD no magic solution for the intro problem, she eased our minds by listening to us and offering suggestions. She was another sympathetic, knowledgeable adult to talk to, and a professional to boot, who knew our boy well and looked at his problems in a similar way. She made Ellen and me feel that there were three of us now, not just two, who were thinking hard and creatively about Walker.

She fully grasped the desperation reverberating through our family: Walker, striving every minute of the day to break through a barrier in his brain; Davy, confused and alarmed by the turmoil in his house; Ellen and I, struggling to keep hope aloft.

Ellen later said that Maureen was like an angel sent to us at the moment we needed her most. And we treated her like one—never saying so, but daily expecting a miracle.

ELEVEN

Yearning

About the time Maureen's light was growing brighter, the homeschooling bulb grew dimmer and dimmer.

The most flagrant sign of this was the way children's videos—which began as a minor break in our routine—gradually became more and more important until, like Ben and Jerry's Cookie Dough ice cream for the over-450-pound community, they became a dominant feature of life.

We resorted to videos in part because of the increasing difficulty of getting Walker to do anything—read, write, work with numbers, put together picture puzzles. So instead of spending a morning begging him, yelling at him, or teasing him into sitting down, I would make a token stab at some activity, give up, put on a video, and frantically grade papers. Since our credit-card debt was mushrooming, Ellen needed to find more freelance work to keep up, even in a virtual-reality, minimum-payment way. I always taught overtime classes, so a perpetual sixteen tons of student papers awaited me in some dark corner of the house.

A nearly typical family tableau: The middle of the night in our living room, all the lights on. Ellen is sitting on the edge of the couch, her fingers flying across her laptop three days past her deadline for a press kit about a men's cologne. I am slumped in my rocker and grading papers that are a week and a half overdue for one of the seven writing classes I am teaching. Walker is in the corner of the dining area, his new permanent bedroom, yelling "Ah! Ah! Ah!" his feet thud-thudding on the floor while he watches "Dumbo." Davy is in the bedroom sleeping, or at least we hope he is sleeping despite our racket.

"What time is it?" I ask.

Ellen looks at the clock on the cable box. "2:27," she says, and looks at me thoughtfully. "If you were a romantic man and you were describing the lift that dabbing your neck with a fragrance gives you, what word would you use?"

"If I were a romantic man, I would probably say the fragrance was 'exhilarating' or maybe 'soul-stirring.' Of course, it would depend on the kind of man you mean. Am I romantic like Cary Grant or am I romantic like Brad Pitt?"

"Oh, Brad Pitt, honey. Brad Pitt absolutely," she says, the slightest hint of a smile disappearing in a flash as she dives back into her work, I sink into mine, and Walker continues his, uninterrupted.

AT NINE, WALKER still adored children's videos, wildly. He brought a new meaning to the term "interactive TV." Our set was like one of those pong paddles that sends a little ball (Walker) bouncing off its surface at the end of a rubber band. He'd stand about twelve feet from the set in the corner of the living room next to the front door. As he watched, he'd wave his hands in the air, arms bent at the elbow, and walk fast toward the TV with his eyes and mouth open wide inhaling heavily with an "ah-ah-ah" sound as he walked, as though every moment of the familiar cartoon had the emotional immediacy of the last five seconds of a Bulls playoff game. Then he'd come right up to the screen until he touched it with his forehead and lips.

After his kiss, he'd walk backwards toward his baseline near the door in exactly the same way; or he'd veer off at an angle across the living room; or he might perform a stunt like running upstairs and watching from the balcony over the living room, then careen down-stairs, run to the back room and listen from there.

En route, he might turn on a radio or throw a ball, but wherever he was in the house, and whatever additional activity he picked up, he always remained tethered to the screen as though by an invisible rubber band and woe to the person who dared turn the television off.

To the uninitiated, all this seemed like one more intolerably zany thing that autism was driving him to do. But to our practiced, sleep-deprived eyes, it seemed a ritual full of interesting nuance. For one thing, all the hard-to-ignore physical movement was, in part, a way to force us *not to ignore him*. It was a way to say, "See how excited I am? Don't you just have to watch this cartoon with me? Aren't we all enjoying this like crazy?" He'd come close to my face while I was reading the newspaper and look into my eyes, grin, and then go back to the screen. For another thing, he could almost never watch a televi-sion show per se, for normal TV would present him constantly with the unexpected. Since the world seemed out of control to him all the time, he needed the reassurance of the predictable. And he had to see only *certain* videos, his favorites—a large collection, to be sure—but still a finite number of them that he saw over and over. Just how many times he had seen any given video was a figure that, for reasons of emotional self-protection, we wouldn't have dared calculate.

And finally, the hammer to our heads, the rewinding. Of course starting any viewing involved his "intro" difficulty (getting past the FBI Warning was sometimes very rough), but he also had trouble leaving his favorite scenes, usually moments of high emotion: the mice showing Cinderella the dress they made for her; the Prince nearly kissing the Little Mermaid. At such scenes, Walker would put both fingers in his ears, blush, look down at the floor and rewind the tape to have the moment again…and again…and again.

Five Disney videos had a special hold on him for over two years. Day-in, day-out, night-in, night-out he'd ask for them by name, shouting their titles until we'd cave and let him see one again. Some-times, sitting with him in front of the set, I speculated about what irre-sistible magnetic power they had. I wondered what drew him to these particular films the way "The Rocky Horror Picture Show" drew its devotees. What would a review of these videos by Walker's hidden self, the Regular Kid, be like?

Walker Reviews Disney

> "The Little Mermaid": A film about an autistic boy growing up on the North Side of Chicago. Of course, certain aspects have been changed to give it a "fairy tale" quality. The boy has been changed to Ariel, a girl whose handicap is that she can't join the human race because she's part fish. Her father, King Triton, is a very realistic figure. Big and affectionate, he's nevertheless a doofus who is prone to sudden fits of anger and is powerless against his daughter's enemies. An especially effective part of the film is when Ariel is mute and can't express herself, not even her love for the prince.
>
> Highlight: The wonderful song, "Part of Your World", in which Ariel sings of how she would like to escape her supposedly beautiful underwater environment and join the race of humans who look like they're having a lot more fun. I strongly recommend a couple of dozen rewinds of this one, if you can get away with it.
>
> "Dumbo": Another film about an autistic boy in Chicago, this time presented as a young elephant in a circus. Though his obvious disability is his enormous ears—the other elephants declare he is "no longer an elephant" because of them—his real handicap is that he's "dumb" and can't speak, even to defend himself. The movie shows that a tiny creature that can talk—Timothy J. Mouse, Dumbo's best friend—has far more power in life than a big kid who can't. But it also holds out the hope that a loyal friend can help a kid overcome big trouble.
>
> Highlight: When Timothy J. Mouse, the wisecracking, upbeat friend, whispers into the Ringmaster's ear when he's sleeping. That Timothy is one very clever Borsht Belt comedian! You'll laugh and laugh!
>
> Another highlight: The sudden appearance of the crows, a crowd of new friends who help give Dumbo confidence.

"Cinderella": This film, clearly about an autistic boy facing great hardship, cleverly masks its real intent by presenting a girl, Cinderella, who dreams of a better life than the dreary one she is trapped in. Though the self-indulgent, over-the-top performance of the wicked stepmother is distracting (I have sometimes ejected the tape during one of her scenes), still the home situation has a certain verisimilitude: the stepsisters get to go out to the party while Cinderella has to stay home.

Highlight: The scene where Cinderella's cute little creature friends sing "We Can Do It" and make a dress for her to go to the ball in. All those friends! All that happiness! It's a terrific rewinding moment!

"Alice in Wonderland": In this classic example of the art of animation the autistic boy stand-in is Alice, a young, homeschooled English girl. While her sister reads some dreary book to her, she begins to dream of a more interesting world of adventure. She gets more than she bargained for, though, and finds herself in a world where she doesn't understand anything anybody says to her. The result is that even though she is doing her best, people are always mad at her. Every time she thinks she's figured out the rules of her crazy world, she finds that the rules have been changed again. The movie does a good job of showing how confusing life is.

Highlight: The greatest rewinding moment of them all: the "Unbirthday Song," a totally funny, crazy episode that has to be seen to be believed. On a personal note: I've gotten into some big trouble rewinding this, but take it from me, it's been worth it.

"The Wind in the Willows": The autistic boy here is Mr. Toad, who dreams of a life of travel and adventure but finds himself stuck with a boring existence under the watchful eyes of old Mac Badger, who keeps Toad from doing anything he really wants to. Toad is hobbled by his obsessions, his manias, that keep him from thinking clearly and get him into big trouble. He loves Mac Badger and his other friends, Ratty and Moley, but he's frustrated by their inability to understand him and what he needs.

Highlight: There's a fantastic scene where a fast-talking lawyer threatens a witness in court. It's very complicated and I used to like to practice this in front of the mirror in the bathroom.

Warning: Following "The Wind in the Willows" on my tape is "The Legend of Sleepy Hollow." I've seen this a few times and it has its moments, but it has no redeeming autistic content and I suggest a quick rewind.

One final suggestion: Any tape with the word "Muppets" in the title is a sure-fire winner. They all contain great songs, terrific characters, and funny sketches, and every one of them presents good Rewind Ops, especially "The Great Muppet Caper."

ANOTHER SIGN OF our gradual disenchantment with home-schooling was the increasing incidence of small cataclysms like our family trip to the Museum of Science and Industry.

When I was growing up in the fifties, the huge sprawling edifice near the University of Chicago had a reputation as a terrific place for kids, not unlike Disneyland, so full of fascinating things that you couldn't see all of them in a month of visits. So I returned again and again with my friends Ed or Buzz or with my father, telling myself I was having a wonderful time. Only as a teenager did I finally admit that for me it was, all along, rather dark, dull, and disappointing.

But maybe Walker and Davy would find it to be the virtual thrill ride most Chicagoans seemed to think it was, and maybe the place had improved.

Things were going well on this bright spring day; that is, we four had gotten through the door and into the main hall without Walker balking at the visual and decibel overload the museum assaulted us with. We could never predict how he would react to a loud public place. Sometimes after parking, walking uneventfully to the door, and paying the entrance fee to a museum, we would find ourselves with a kicking, screaming boy yelling "Go home!" Other times he seemed to enjoy loud places. In a crowd at Wrigley Field or in the loud atrium of the Field Museum, he often seemed to lose himself in the noise and the anonymity crowds create. So getting through the door and into the dark center of the museum without an explosion was a good sign.

All of a sudden, just as we were about to veer off to look at an airplane, Walker yelled "POOP!" So down to the lower level of the museum we all went, we three boys into the men's room—a comically huge place with a surreal number of options—and emerged success-fully a few minutes later into the large, crowded, circular lobby just outside. When we met up with Ellen, without any warning, Walker ambushed me, biting the collar of my T-shirt and tugging me downward. I pulled him off my shirt and grabbed both his hands.

"CAR!" he screamed, falling away from me then leaping up into my face.

"Sit down!" I whisper-growled as only I knew how to do.

He lunged to grab me around the neck. He sank his teeth into my shirt near the neck. I forced him to the floor where I whisper-growled at him some more and noticed a crowd gathering. Into my head popped the thought that this looked like child abduction—a boy clutching and biting in self-defense, a big man forcing the boy to go somewhere against the boy's will.

Surely no exhibit in the museum could top this.

The people around us, a crescent-shaped wall of gapers, was a blur to me except for two lucky enormous women in front who, like two Chevy Suburbans stopped to view a wreck on the highway, were blocking the angle of vision of those behind them. They wore brightly-colored sweatshirts and had fat faces and fat necks and fat arms and blank stares and whispered to each other without taking their eyes off us. They were ladies who would have something to talk about when they get back home and somebody asked, "Well, how was the museum?"

There was no time for my mantra—Ellen and I had to make some quick decisions.

We shouted our discussion of our next move in little telegraphic bursts—"You and Davy"…"We stay"…"One hour?"…"One and a half"…"North entrance"—over Walker's screams and in front of our attentive audience. I'd take Walker out in the car, drive around, and meet up with them at the entrance in an hour and a half.

So we split, Ellen and Davy going off to an exhibit, the child abductor and his victim struggling and grappling with each other up the stairs. As we did this, it began to dawn on me for the first time just how far we were from the entrance to the museum—a couple of football fields away?—and just how many people would be staring at us.

So I avoided eye contact with everyone and just concentrated on containment. I lifted him, dragged him, pushed him; I tried humor, then crazy threats. I considered the classic TV police show move of pulling one of his arms up behind his back, pushing him forward from behind, and whispering menace in his ear. But Walker was so out of control he seemed to be capable of breaking his own arm rather than cooperate. I wanted to put my hand over his mouth, for he was screaming "CAAAAR!" as loud as he could, and it was very audible even in this, the loudest museum in the city. But doing so would be the definitive child abductor move. All this time I was keeping his mouth away from my clothes, for he was determined to bite me anywhere he could. Even now, in all this excitement, my old enemy Anxiety reared its ugly head and I thought, My God, what will I do when he's bigger and stronger?

Holding him against my body and pushing his face away from my neck, I inched him through the exit and to the Escort at the far end of the huge parking lot. And though he'd been yelling "CAR!" almost continually, when the time arrived for him actually to get in, he screamed and gripped the door and the edge of the roof and kicked me in the stomach, Jimmy Cagney about to go to the chair. At this moment I spotted, out of the corner of my eye, a policeman walking by. I thought, *Oh, no!* but he looked at me and nodded sympathetically: he knew exactly what was going on.

Walker was now in the back seat, thrashing around and screaming, the rear door child lock, this time, in place. With a kick, he dislodged the change holder between the two front seats and the coins flew all over the car. I started yelling, "STOP! STOP IT NOW!" and slapping his leg and shaking my fist at him. We drove out of the parking lot, and my goal was just to drive around aimlessly, usually a soothing maneuver.

We drove for miles up and down Lake Shore Drive with the radio on. I had tears streaming down my face as he continued to kick and scream for another forty-five minutes or so. Even when he started to quiet down, I was still on edge, still worried another offensive could break out. When the looking-out-the-window-at-the-lake-and-listening-to-the-music stage finally arrived, I pulled off the Drive and started cruising around the nearby University of Chicago.

By now a monster of self-pity, I thought about the time when I was about Walker's age, maybe a year or two older, when my mother had taken me for a stroll around the campus.

It was a sunny autumn afternoon when the ivy was turning color and the leaves from the giant trees all around were falling. She pointed out Ida Noyes Hall, where she met my father at a dance when they were both students there in the 1940s; she was a freshman, he a junior. She talked about my father's brother, Donald, who had been a nuclear physicist here and worked with Enrico Fermi. Uncle Donald was a hero to me. I dreamed of growing up to be a physicist like him, and I tried to cultivate a Future Einstein image by using big words and acting inscrutable, especially around girls.

I walked around the campus on that afternoon listening to my mother, feeling proud of my family, and wanting to grow up fast so I could be tall, wear a sweater, carry books under my arm, and walk through the doors of serious old stone buildings such as the ones I was looking at all around me.

But there was to be no recapitulating this visit with my own son, who might well remember this day as a horrible moment of despair when he couldn't talk to his parents about the panic and misery shooting through him.

THAT NIGHT, AFTER the boys had gone to bed, Ellen and I sat on the couch and thrashed out the reasons for Walker's protracted hysteria. There was the Too Much Noise and Too Many People Hypothesis, a good standby, but not reliable, for sometimes a surging multitude seemed to relax him. There was the Frustration Over Not Being Able to Express Something On His Mind Hypothesis, always a possibility, especially when biting was involved, for that signaled a desire to speak. But this one-man riot of his was over the top, even for him. There was the Mysterious Chemical Shift in the Brain, and its twin, an Untrackable Malfunctioning of His Mental Wiring Hypotheses. Both explanations were oddly attractive that night, for they'd let us off the hook; we could shrug and say, "Who knew?"

But a new explanation occurred to us, a fascinating one, but admittedly not much more helpful than the others, one we quickly called the "Location, Location, Location Hypothesis." Walker had held it together until he was deep in the bowels of the museum, but once in the basement and the geometric middle of the gargantuan building, far from an exit, and he *had* to get out. We knew that in whatever building he found himself he gravitated toward the extreme corners. If we entered someone's house for the first time, Walker would instantly dash for a corner; we found him once in a basement, once at the back of a closet on a top floor. Even at home he took up positions near the front and back doors and in the corner of our upstairs bedroom.

It was as though he was, emotionally at least, perpetually defending the Alamo, never to be outflanked by attacking soldiers and prepared to face anything coming at him.

It seemed to be related to his endless study of *Above Chicago*, the lovely picture book that Ellen had bought for him several months before. Lying in bed, leaning over the aerial photographs of the city, he'd stare and stare at areas he knew about on the ground, visualizing his position on the planet at every moment. He seemed to have lodged in his head at all times a map of where he was, a kind of mental GPS device, and as he walked through the museum, he was able to visualize his distance from the exits as well as his distance from the corners, and all his alarms went off.

But beyond all our theories, his long museum detonation represented something new and alarming, something over our heads. Was he deeply miserable? Did he need—it made me nauseated even to think of the word—more *structure?*

Did he need, even want, to go to school?

THE TALL, THIN, good-looking boy with blood on his face was flanked by two angry men, one very fat and one very skinny, who were gripping him by the elbows and hustling him towards me. I stepped to the side of the narrow hall and flattened myself against the wall to let the three of them pass.

"What was that?" I asked. I was visiting a private school for autistic children on the North Side of Chicago, and a teacher was giving me a tour.

"Oh, that's Ricky. He must be having trouble today," my docent explained, a look of embarrassment on her face.

"Where are they taking him?"

"Probably to the time-out room."

"Could I see that?"

"There's nothing much to see, really."

"My wife would like me to take a look at that," I said, giving my helpless, just-following-orders shrug—my signature dodge—and started to follow the struggling threesome. They took him around the corner to a small hallway. The fat guy pushed the boy up against the wall while the thin guy opened an oversized steel door that had a small square window in the middle of it. Then the two of them pushed Ricky into a room with padding on the walls, floor, and ceiling and slammed the door shut. Despite all the padding, Ricky managed thunderous pounding on the other side of the door. My spinmeister interpreted: "This doesn't happen very often. The time-out room is only used for very extreme situations, and someone must stand directly outside the room the entire time a child is in there."

All the special ed horror stories I had ever read in the newspaper or heard from other parents raced through my mind—about children locked in "time out" for entire days, about special ed classes held in washrooms because of overcrowding, about classes "taught" by bus drivers enlisted to watch over the kids, about the rape of a little girl under her desk while the teacher read a newspaper in the front of the room. I thought of Walker and how much trouble he could be and how tempted a harried teacher would be to pitch him into the slammer and throw away the key; of how easy it would be to misinterpret his wild attempts at communication; of how an inattentive or overworked teacher could think he was "bad" and needed to be "taught a lesson."

Yet this school was *highly recommended!* People paid *lots of money* to enroll their children here instead of the public school!

As I walked away with the tour guide and the sound of Ricky's fury faded in the distance, I wondered what Walker would think of this place. When he was of pre-school age, and we were still in our Hopeful-About-Our-Boy-Genius Stage, Ellen took him to an open house at a local private school. As they were approaching the big brick ivy-covered building, Walker read aloud a word above the door and shouted it merrily: "School! School! School!"

Inside, as Ellen picked up a brochure from a table, Walker smiled and jumped in place holding her hand. She turned and spotted a nearby mother who nodded slightly in Walker's direction and whispered something to a teacher. The teacher glanced at him, turned to the mother, and said, without bothering to lower her voice, "Oh, don't worry. He wouldn't last here more than a day."

This was the fatal disparity: Walker's high hopes about school (his beloved "Sesame Street" treated school as childhood's core magnificent experience) versus school's dim view of him. It was entirely possible, I thought as I listened to the woman speak of the wonders of her Autism Jail, that Walker's Big Bird-inspired view of school had only intensified over the homeschooling years, that he envisioned Davy going off each morning to a cozy wonderland of friendship and fun.

What would Walker think of the scene I'd just witnessed? And of the unused and unusable "gym" that would be ready "some day"? Of the doorway to the school, monitored by a woman in a glass cage who commandeered the buzzer to the outside world, an entrance that reminded me of the infamous Lincoln Towing yard on Clark Street where angry drivers tried to retrieve their cars?

Yet here I was, touring a maximum security elementary school because of one terrible fact: Walker was a runner. No one could tell when he might simply *bolt*—dash across an intersection, jump out of a car, skip into an alley. When we ran along the lakefront together, he usually hugged the wire fence separating us from Lake Shore Drive. He loved the Doppler *whoosh* of oncoming cars just a few feet away, of the sensation that the cars were coming *at* him. I knew this fence well, where the gaps were, where it stopped abruptly, and a sensor seemed to beep in my brain fifty yards before danger. Then with friendliness or sternness or hysteria, I steered him away from the fence. I was, every second, all over him. I was his father, his teacher, his friend, but I was also his tense U.S. Marshall escorting him from one incarceration situation to another.

My ultra vigilance could seem crazy to an observer. Outdoors, I was always within arm's length of him, ready to lunge and grab, no matter how fast or slow he ran. If he halted to kiss the wall of Marshall Field's, to stare up at the sky, to jump in place and spit on the sidewalk, I stood right by his shoulder and tried to look casual. If he reversed direction and retraced his steps for twenty yards, stopped, then turned back again, so did I. Yet despite his zaniness, Walker had such a sunny demeanor, such good looks, and such a cooperative air, that he didn't *seem* to need this kind of guarding. Sometimes a relative or friend would say something along the lines of "Hey, take it easy. He's just having fun. Don't be so nervous."

But whenever we let our guard down, something happened. On a chilly Saturday morning in May, Walker, dressed in just pajamas, discovered that one of the three deadbolts in our front door was unlocked and made a break for it. Running at full tilt and shouting for him to stop, I caught him just before he reached busy Belmont Avenue. While I was tugging the happy jailbird back home (he was laughing the whole way), a neighbor said to me, in all seriousness, "Why don't you just let him go and see what happens?"

I knew Walker longed to get out of his parental handcuffs, and we sought to give him, whenever possible, if not the freedom of the nine-year-old he was, at least a little bit more slack to move about the grounds. On the Fourth of July in 1995, the four of us were at a friend's house for a picnic. There were children everywhere and Walker seemed very happy and comfortable, doing what the child developers call "parallel play," not exactly joining in but staying with the kids and keeping busy. The bratwurst and beer and adult conversation were in the back yard; the kids were in the house and in the front yard. Ellen and I took turns pretending to be parents at ease, one of us chatting and eating while the other kept watch near Walker.

He was in the basement with several kids and doing so well that I stepped into the backyard while Ellen was there—a rare public appearance of both of us, Clark Kent *and* Superman. Our friend, a mother of four boys, said, "Wow, here the two of you are at the same time! You know, Walker's doing real well. He's not going anywhere. The kids will keep an eye on him. Relax." She said this with the knowing confidence of a parent with a greater number of children than we.

I talked for a little while like a grownup, all the while wondering and worrying. I ate a whole hamburger. I drank a whole beer. Then I casually wandered back into the basement. He wasn't there. I went upstairs. He wasn't there either. Out the front door and into the yard, I looked all around: many kids, but no Walker. "Have you seen Walker?" I asked a little girl. "Oh, he went that way with Michael." *He went that way with who?!* She pointed down the block toward busy Addison Street. I took off running.

When I reached the corner, I looked down a very, very long stretch of sun-baked sidewalk along Addison, a street with low 1960s-era brick bungalows lining it as far as the eye could see. About two blocks ahead I spotted a boy, but not Walker. Could that be Michael? I sprinted forward, yelling "Michael! Michael!" He stopped and waited for me.

"Have you seen Walker?" I asked.

"That's him there," he said, and pointed further ahead. I looked down the sidewalk, but didn't see anybody.

"Where?"

"There. That's him there, see?" he said, still pointing.

I looked again. Far, far ahead, about four full blocks away, I saw a figure. "Is that Walker, way down there?" I asked, bending low.

"Uh-huh. I couldn't keep up with him."

I was off again, shouting "WALKER! STOP!" over and over. Then I discovered something: it's impossible to yell as loud as you can while running as fast as you can. You have to stop and yell or run and keep quiet. So I just ran.

Ahead of Walker I could make out what I feared most, a stop light—the first traffic-heavy intersection he had met. On and on I ran, my brain saying Go! Go! Go! but my legs seeming to move slower and slower. Walker got to the light before I did, hesitated, but didn't turn around to look at me.

Reaching him—almost toppling over him—as a car sped by the edge of the curb where he stood, I gasped for air like an unathletic, panic-stricken, forty-six-year-old English teacher.

SO WALKER WAS a runner, yes. Despite that fact we wanted for him the kind of school he yearned for—a real one.

But the still, small voice of despair told us that such a place didn't really exist.

TWELVE

The Apocalypse

For one thing, the woman was too small and pretty, the college cheerleader they boost to the top of the pyramid. For another, her school was too good: a large, old, pleasant red brick house near the lake, its front door buzzerless—no guard house, no battlements, in fact actually *unlocked*, as though the school were in Mayberry, not on the North Side of Chicago. Energetic-looking young teachers in homey, carpeted classrooms hovered over quiet children at desks and tables.

So even before Ellen and I sat down in Laurie Bushman's office—after a few minutes' observation of the school—I concluded dourly that Walker wouldn't last a day here. *It looks great,* I thought, *but he's a runner and a screamer and biter. And he's strong. They wouldn't be ready for him.*

But as Ellen and I launched into The Speech—unabridged version—Laurie punctuated our oral history with words like "wonderful" and "good for you" and "terrific." When we got to our basic heresy—that everything he did was communication of some kind—she, like Maureen, agreed heartily.

"He sounds just great. I'd love to meet him," she said.

I hesitated and glanced at Ellen. "Walker's big for his age and can be loud. He can suddenly just take off. Do you think you could handle that?"

"Oh," she laughed. "You caught us at a peaceful moment. It can get pretty wild here."

But do you have anybody like Walker Hughes? I thought.

"Could I see your time-out room?" I asked.

"Our what?"

"You know, the room where you put kids who are getting too wild."

"Oh, no, we don't believe in anything like that." Suddenly there emerged a more steely tone of voice, an experienced note of authority. "We don't have anything like a separate [gestured quotation marks in the air] 'punishment room.' Just like you say, even a shouting child is trying to communicate something. We don't want to shut him down and just cast him out. Autistic kids are desperate to communicate and we want to show them that we understand how they feel."

She explained that they had a graduated system, ranging from the child putting his head on his desk and counting to ten, all the way to the child sitting off away from the other children, behind a screen, but never alone. A teacher always remained with the child, and they took turns if the situation became too stressful.

I still had my doubts. Could this gentle strategy really stand up to Walker's storms? Could this quiet school, with a supportive, encouraging ethos like in an ideal homeschool (with the ungainly acronym PACTT, Parents Allied with Children and Teachers for Tomorrow) really handle him? But the attitude was so *right*. One thing was clear—this school was worth shooting for.

IT CAN BE a depressingly long way from parents deciding which expensive, private, special school they think is right for their developmentally disabled child and actually getting the public school system to fund the parents' choice. Under the Americans with Disabilities Act, all children have a right to an "appropriate" education, even if that means underwriting a pricey private school. But the local school district can resist the parents mightily, insist on the accuracy of its own self-serving label, and send the whole process into endless, agonizing litigation.

Ellen had a plan: find a psychologist who could see him essentially the way we did, pay for our own private evaluation, and then approach the public school with all our ducks in a row. Such a plan called for diplomacy and people skills. It called for charm and the ability to keep one's head and a smile on one's face while being patronized. So it called for me to stay out of it. But the plan meant that we would have to run through another gauntlet of developmental police, deliver "The Speech" several more times to various skeptical experts, and then face a phalanx of Chicago Public School people with our suggestion to place Walker at PACTT School.

Ellen's great find was a somewhat enlightened child psychologist, an autism specialist, who didn't flinch in horror at our initial decision to homeschool Walker. This psychologist accepted his "atypicalness" and thought our child-rearing decisions had been reasonable. But even she had her limitations. After testing him, she reported that Walker's IQ was "below 50." How, we asked, did his IQ plunge from 129 at age two to "below 50" at age ten? She had no explanation, and—this was the most frustrating thing to us—she didn't find the question particularly interesting. Why was he able to speak complete sentences on rare occasions? She didn't know and didn't really care.

Again and again we ran into professionals in the field who didn't find Walker—or autism itself for that matter—*interesting*. The matter was cut and dried, they seemed to say. Autistic children are essentially the same; despite their differences, the label defined them. Manage the kid safely and comfortably, learn the jargon of the field, and try to get the child to learn a few life skills—this was about all a parent could achieve for a "low-functioning" autistic.

The pediatrician who examined Walker in this process was an excellent example of the breed. When we reached the portion of the biography where we told of our decision to try homeschooling, she was shocked, *shocked!* It was our *obligation* to enroll him as soon as we knew there was trouble, just as she had enrolled her own learning disabled child.

She instructed Walker to strip down to his underpants, turned off the light in the examining room, and proceeded for a full ten minutes to examine him all over his body with an ultraviolet light. She didn't explain what this was for, but we knew: it was to detect subcutaneous bruising from child abuse. She *knew* only Mommie Dearest types, voodoo ritualists, satanic cultists, or cross-eyed, gun-totin', tobaccy-chewin' survivalists would keep their child hidden from the school authorities. She *knew* nobody could live with the shouting, jumping, wild kid in front of her without beating him up regularly. Her UV apparatus turned out to be ninety percent of the exam. And when she finished, though she found no bruising, we were not off the hook as far as she was concerned.

Her body language, her reserve, her unwillingness to listen to much of anything we had to say told us clearly: *She knew outlaws when she saw them.*

But at the end of this process, we had it: an evaluation that explicitly suggested Walker should attend PACTT School and that the school system should pay for it. Despite this impressive pile of paper, Ellen and Maureen and I prepared ourselves for punishing skepticism and obduracy from the Chicago Public School evaluators. We even had a game plan for the big meeting: Maureen and Ellen would do most of the talking; short-tempered Bob would nod and smile and say things like, "Oh, you are so right!"

Then something happened that took our breath away: the panel of public school representatives were *nice*. They were more than nice; they practically stood up and cheered us. The six evaluators and administrators sitting around the table on that sunny afternoon in the early spring competed with each other in their praise of our parenting, our wisdom, even our choice of homeschooling. We wanted to hug every one of them, we were so happy. We were also baffled: the Developmental Police, far from blocking our path, had given us a motorcade to our destination.

Thus Walker, at age ten, began his school career. Each day that April after putting him on the bus, Ellen and I expected The Call—*I'm sorry, Mr. and Mrs. Hughes. Walker threw a chair through a window. I'm afraid he's just not suited for us here. He needs to be in a more tightly structured environment.* But the first day passed, then the second, then whole weeks, and The Call never came. He must have been difficult, but we never heard a negative word about him.

Walker now got up each morning eager to get on the bus and shouted happily "PACTT School! PACTT School!" Ellen and I were able to breathe during the day: she could take on more freelance writing work; I could shift my teaching schedule to mornings, which I had all along preferred. And Davy finally had an older brother who went to school and didn't stay home with Dad "having fun."

Life was instantly better.

AROUND THAT TIME life improved for another reason, too. While visiting with some friends, we made a small discovery with huge quality-of-life implications.

Anne and Peter's house was everything ours dreamed of being. Like ours it had a vaulted ceiling with crossbeams overhead, a mezzanine bedroom that looked down on the living room, and a kitchen only a toy truck's throw from above. Guests sat on the couch and chatted or looked at the blazing fire or gazed out the front windows. But unlike ours the walls had no tattoo-deep images of small human hands, the hardwood floors had a *finish*. And the front windows! When you looked out of them you weren't checking out what an unleashed pit bull was doing in your postage stamp-sized front yard, no! What you saw was a serene little lake surrounded by fir trees—no boats, no people, no Ford Explorers speeding backwards to seize parking spaces.

All four of us were in this lovely place one cold winter afternoon. It had been a rough time getting there. It was a one and a half hour's drive away for normals, two and a half hours for us. Walker was at a stage in which he shouted impatiently at every momentary pause in our forward motion—at red lights, traffic slow-downs, stop signs. Gridlock was unthinkable. When the shouting got too bad, I'd pull over to the side of the road.

With cars speeding by a few feet away I would hold him by the shoulders and look into his face: "We won't move until you stop shouting, Walker."

"Shouting!" he'd yell back.

"No, say, 'I'll stop shouting, Dad.'"

"Stop shouting Dad."

"No, look at me! We won't get in the car until you stop!"

"Stop."

And so on and so on.

None of this trouble in transit compared to the overarching anxiety about the Getting Out of the Car Intro: he could simply refuse to budge when we got there, and we'd have to turn around and go back.

But we took the risk because we knew Walker liked Peter and Anne very much. Anne was quite possibly the most empathetic person we knew, and Walker clearly thought of Peter as a friend. Once when they were leaving our house, Walker tugged on Peter's hand and said, "You stay here."

We had guessed right. Walker ran into their house and up the stairs to the far corner of the mezzanine bedroom and Davy entertained us all with his stories about the "Fekudonts," his name for a world of imaginary characters of his own making, a race of creatures with ancestry, vivid habitats and adventures, his own eight year old's *Lord of the Rings.*

As always when at someone's house, Ellen and I only paid partial attention to our hosts. *He's not making any noise up there,* we both were thinking. *What's he doing?* We were like the cavalry in an old western who knew the real trouble began when the drumbeats stopped. So we nervously ate cheese and crackers and nervously laughed and checked on him every five minutes.

After a while we started to hear a rhythmic *thud—thud—thud* coming from above, accompanied by giggling and shouting. All of us

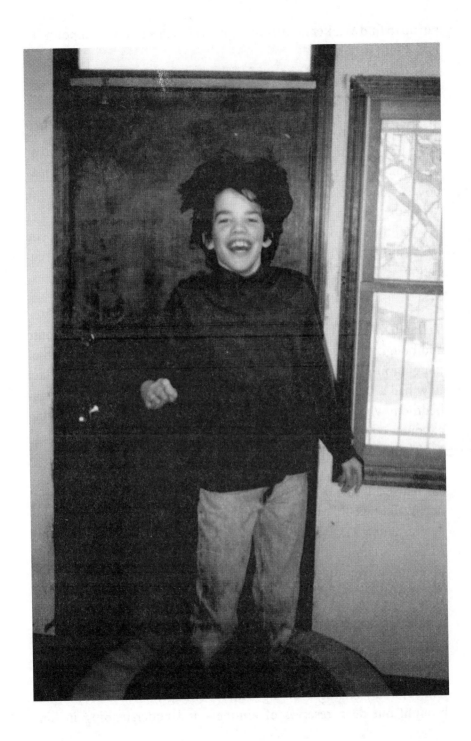

ran up to find Walker bouncing high on a small exercise trampoline he had found up there.

"Wow, Walker!" Anne said. "That's great! Go, man!" Then she explained to us that she had read how jumping on a trampoline releases enzymes or hormones or something that race through the bloodstream and create a Zen-like harmony of mind and body. So she'd bought one, jumped on it a few times, decided all that serenity was more than she could take, and never used it again. Walker, however, took to it like it was a ride at Disneyland. He was wild with delight and there was no stopping him.

We all watched him with smiles on our faces. Peter said, "Well, you know, as Oscar Wilde said, 'Every gentleman should have some occupation.'"

THE NEXT DAY I went to the Sportmart a few blocks from our house and bought trampoline number one. It changed our lives. Instead of jumping in place on the floor right above the tenant's head, Walker now had a trampolining spot on the third floor in the corner of our bedroom where he could watch videos and jump without bothering anyone.

The trampoline partially revived the World of Guys that we once had. Davy, standing on the bed, would throw a basketball to me. I'd catch it and throw it to Walker, who was leaping high on the trampoline. Walker would catch it mid-air, come down, bounce up and throw it, mid-jump, to Davy. The three of us could go on and on like this with endless variations: throwing the ball over a rafter, down the steps, bouncing it over the bed.

Most of the rule changes were of Walker's invention. Davy, by now, had a clear idea of Walker's disability, and treated him with patience. He'd take his cue from me, and go with the flow of the game. He seemed to have a deep sense of how Walker was feeling at any given moment, and would say to us: "I feel like Walker lots of times, but I can talk about my feelings." Living with his strange, raucous brother had brought out deep reserves of kindness and understanding in him.

When I was a child, I could barely muster the sympathy to think of the "starving children in India;" I certainly never exhibited anything like the patience Davy called upon every day.

Jumping on the trampoline clearly *was* Walker's new occupation. It was a form of vertical running that could be done in the house no matter the weather. But it soon became clear that Walker could jump higher and more continuously than the trampoline manufacturer had in mind. We became accustomed to the loud *toing!* of the breaking spring upstairs followed by the *ping!* of the broken spring hitting the wall. I'd wait until just before he was jumping on a flat canvas on the floor before going back to Sportmart with the pieces. "I'm sorry," I'd say to the clerk. "It must have been a defective one." And for no cost they'd give me another one.

But I knew they'd get suspicious (or I'd feel too embarrassed) if I tried to do this forever. So I developed a "three strikes" rule: I'd allow myself to hit the same store just three times. Then I'd drive to another one and pay for a new trampoline and begin the replacement game over again. Ellen and I disagree on how many trampolines there were: I say twenty-nine; she says thirty. As time went by, I stacked jagged three-foot circles of steel and canvas in the back yard so I could raid them for replacement springs.

Our "discovery" of trampolines was one many parents of autistic children make. Somehow, in some way, jumping stimulates and relaxes at the same time. Even watching videos while jumping is a common practice. But we knew our wild, ecstatic athlete was *sui generis:* nobody leaped with such happy abandon, nobody smiled with such joy and pride at the amazed reaction of others.

ONE NIGHT AFTER pulling into the garage after class, I stepped into the middle of our backyard and my spirits fell. I was standing in a nearly triangular space between the house and our small, nearly triangular brick garage, both of them pushed into their shape by the diagonal line of the alley behind the house. The yard aspired to a décor principle that can best be described as "redneck feng shui." Though it was, admittedly, too small to hold 1970s-era automobiles with their engines missing, defunct washing machines, rusted-out water heaters, or twisted sections of barbed-wire fencing, it did contain second-tier stuff—a wheelbarrow with a deflated tire, an unusable basketball net, old flower pots, dirt, weeds, chopped-up sections of a tree trunk, a huge hole dug by Davy, and a monstrous, half-dead "tree of heaven" (its actual name!) that stank, provided little shade, and worked relentlessly at propagating itself year-round by raining down branches and mysterious sticks and tiny green tufts of seeds.

The backyard was very, very low on our list of priorities, but this didn't stop us from fantasizing about what somebody with money and time could do with it. We called it "an ideal urban space." We rhapsodized about a marvelous deck and garden and silently shook our heads over how such things were out of our reach.

I stood there miserably that night and thought about how the yard was a good image of my out-of-control life; about how the exhausting attention to Walker left little time for even the minimal homeowner stuff; about how my nightly entrance through the back door always reminded me of the intros to medical shows on TV: the urgent music, the doctors and nurses rushing down corridors, the gurney with a bleeding patient slamming through double doors into surgery.

Then I heard shouts coming, oddly enough, from high above my head. *God, what now?* I thought. I stepped back into the garage and out to the alley to get an angle of vision to see the top floor. Three stories up in our mezzanine bedroom was a transom window, very bright in the darkness, positioned over an unused door to yet another never-to-be-built deck. Suddenly, a grinning face appeared, then—*poof!*—vanished. A split second later it bounced into view again, this time a little higher so the shoulders were visible, then again disappeared. Walker was leaping on his tenth or twelfth trampoline so high and shouting *"Ah! Ah! Ah! Ah!"* so loudly and merrily that anyone passing through the alley or even driving by on Clark Street fifty yards away could take in the show.

I smiled. The boy could be so *happy.* For a minute I was psychically airlifted out of my backyard and its silly symbolism. Walker seemed to be saying to anybody who'd listen: *See me! Isn't it great to jump? To enjoy your legs? To bounce way up and look out this high window? And freak out your dad? Wake up and look around! There's fun to be had!*

For a delicious moment I visited the small, seldom-seen spa in my head, the place where I stop and smell the roses and count my blessings. Almost every day he offered to take me there despite the fog of worry over my face. Tonight he broke through with his most indisputably amazing gift—his delight.

THAT SUMMER AFTER Walker's first couple of months at PACTT had ended, Walker grew increasingly agitated. We had returned to our homeschooling routine (which was hardly a routine at all), but he became more and more difficult, more addicted to videos, more restless.

In hindsight, Walker's performance outside the coffee shop that steamy night in August should have tipped us off that disaster was coming. But we couldn't see it at the time—our ideology permitted no negative thinking. We were fanatics on the point: Predicting catastrophe breeds catastrophe. We knew that keeping hope aloft was a very tricky business and not for the faint of heart. Ellen and I were like circus performers who keep smiling while juggling increasingly weird and dangerous items: first a ball, then a dagger, then a torch.

He and I were walking back from Blockbuster Video and having a rough time of it. That summer he had developed a habit of lying down on the sidewalk, flat on his back, and refusing to get up. I'd stand over him, coaxing him and tugging at his arm. Sometimes he'd get up after only a few seconds; sometimes it took a full minute or two. I'd crouch down on the sidewalk next to him and alternate words of encouragement with threats, all the time acting casual. This was my goal, to act casual.

Such a sight is alarming in a small town or suburb, but in our neighborhood it took much more to hit the threshold of pedestrian surprise. On the two-block walk to the video store we might encounter—actually *step over*—many characters stretched out in various positions on the sidewalk: spiky-haired kids begging (derisively!) for money; groups of people standing and sitting at storefronts; an occasional lost soul sleeping deeply who is mortally offended if awakened and asked, "Can I help you?"

Walker had already hit the ground three times when he did it again in front of a coffee house, aptly named "Scenes." This was a cozy-looking cafe with a theater theme. It had bookshelves lined with plays, and I imagined—though I couldn't know for sure since I had never actually set foot in it—that actors and would-be actors hung out there. It had giant windows almost to the ground, and you could see attractive young men and women sitting inside, doubtless discussing Ibsen and Chekhov and enjoying their evenings in a carefree, childless, and I hoped, meaningless and shallow way.

Walker lay there next to the window. I stood over him facing the window and kept the crowd on the narrow sidewalk from tripping over him. Inches away on the other side of the glass sat two young women looking at us quizzically. In my Cosby-esque way, I tried joking him into getting up and moving on. I tugged lightly on his arm, but he seized my hand with both of his and pulled me down as hard as he could. As I grabbed him by his shoulders and pulled him up, he tore at my T-shirt and ripped it down the middle. Then he bit my hand and screamed. This was way off the scale. He was tall and very strong for a ten-year-old (after all, he exercised in one way or another almost every waking moment), and I began to wonder if I could contain him at all.

Our struggle went on and on. He jerked away from me, I lost my balance, and we both slammed the window. I turned and pushed him up against the glass and, like a TV cop, grasped him by his shirt near the throat and tried to "talk some sense into him." The coffee klatchers were now on their feet, staring.

We had reached the threshold of surprise.

Later that night Ellen and I tried to figure out what had happened. We knew it was a bad time for Walker. He was in the no-man's land of the break between his summer program at the Jewish Community Center and the beginning of his first full term at PACTT. He was accustomed to the stimulation and structure of planned activities and was now cut adrift. He might also have a headache or feel ill, but unless he had a fever, we would never know it. At the least, we reasoned, he had to be very uncomfortable with the heat. Day after day the oven-like temperature both inside and outside our house combined with his trampolining and constant movement must be driving him crazy. He and Davy had the only air conditioner we owned in their bedroom, but Walker insisted on sleeping in the dining room with the light on over his head. We placed two fans near his nest on the floor, but hot air blowing in the face has its limits.

So, we calculated: unrelieved physical discomfort *plus* uncertainty about what was coming up next in his life *plus* inability to express any of his feelings equaled ... well, shaking your dad to pieces in the street. It was his way of saying *Change the way I feel, dammit!*

But the Thursday evening scene at Scenes, we soon learned, was just a rehearsal.

ON THE FOLLOWING Sunday night at nine both boys were in bed. Davy was in his cool, quiet bedroom; Walker was asleep in the dining room on his mattress, soothed by the bright light shining on his eyelids, the drone of the propeller-like fans, and the racket of cars and people outside our open windows.

Ellen and I, seated on the couch trying to hear the TV, all of a sudden saw Walker leap up and start jumping in place in the corner, shouting *ah! ah! ah!* as loudly as he could. He picked up his small radio and held it high in the air, still jumping. "Don't, Walker!" I shouted. He threw it across the room, hitting the opposite wall and sending the batteries flying. Before I could reach him, he had swept everything off the table onto the floor and was stepping up onto a chair. I grabbed him, pinned him to the floor, and tried to say soothing things to him while he bucked and tried to slam his head against my face and bite me anywhere he could.

Ellen and I looked at each other in fright: This was a whole new level of mayhem, some dimension of trouble we knew nothing about.

I let him go and he ran, yelling, to the back door, and the jumping started again. We followed him, cornered him, and tried to speak quietly: "Do you feel sick, Walker? … Do you want to see a doctor?… Do you want some water?…Do you have a headache?…Does your stomach hurt?…Your tooth?" But we were speaking to a boy who was jumping so high that his head nearly brushed the low ceiling and who had a wild, angry look in his eyes we'd never seen before. If we tried to touch him, he'd lash out at us, biting, kicking, hitting. If we let him alone, he'd tear through the house screaming and throwing things, running up and down the stairs, standing on the dining room table and slamming down on the floor.

He was relentless. We were used to his usual night-time outbursts; they were by comparison short and punctuated by stretches of peace. But now one hour passed, then another. By eleven thirty Ellen suggested we call the doctor and get him checked into a hospital. I objected: "What are they going to do? This will pass. We have to give him more time."

After another hellish hour, we decided to telephone our tenant downstairs and let him know what was going on.

"I don't hear anything," he told Ellen. "It's not bothering me." For a second we were stunned by this reaction to what must have sounded like D-Day upstairs. Who knew Mike, our tenant, was a saint? But there was no time to contemplate the mystery of human kindness—Walker was still in full throttle. This time it was I who suggested calling the hospital. "No," Ellen said, with tears in her eyes, "it's late. He's got to sleep some time."

No he didn't. When he'd kept it up for another half hour, I said: "I've got an idea. I'll put him in the car and we'll take a nice cool drive and he'll fall asleep."

In the car Walker's rigid limbs relaxed a bit. A refreshing rain started to fall, and so I opened the windows, turned on some classical music, and took a deep breath. Walker put his fingers in his ears—a sure sign that he was listening to the music intently—and I began to settle down along with him. I took a circuitous, time-killing route, and ended up at a 7-Eleven in Evanston. There I discovered a fascinating factoid about myself: the voice in my head that says, "Wouldn't some chocolate be good right about now, Bob?" cannot be muted even by an emergency. I bought the biggest, most overpriced Häagen-Dazs ice cream bars I could find, and we ate them with pleasure.

At three a.m. we were walking up our high back stairs into the house, and I was congratulating myself on having saved the day. Walker was now a new man, contented and ready for bed. But as we stood on the landing and I started to put the key in the lock, he shouted, *"No house today!"* and grabbed my face, sending my glasses flying over the side to the ground and grasped my T-shirt by the collar (a tactic of now proven effectiveness) and tore it down the middle.

Nothing had changed!

By about four a.m. he was asleep, but two hours later he was up again shouting and running back and forth through the house. There was no question now, no discussion: he had to go to the psych ward.

A week followed in which Ellen and I could still hear his screams in our heads even though he was not in the house. The staff at the hospital were amazed at him. He continued to jump and yell that morning long after we'd dropped him off and they had medicated him. We were only allowed to visit him once a day, and we worried: Would he feel abandoned? Would he distrust us in the future? Would his fragile sense of security be smashed? But we also felt guilty relief that he was in safe hands, somebody else's safe hands. We breathed freely, went out with Davy to a non-McDonald's restaurant and saw a non-animated movie. We were like *real* people.

The psychiatrist at the hospital said Walker had had a "psychotic episode"—a dry, unevocative term that wrapped the whole horrible experience in an aura of intelligibility but provided no helpful explanation beyond what we'd already guessed. Davy, who had spent that night awake and scared to death listening to his brother thunder through the house and his parents talk helplessly, had a better word for it, one that captured the true family impact. He said it was "the Apocalypse."

WHEN WALKER RETURNED home, the school year started up again and Walker was more like himself. No one could explain why he fell apart. Some guesses were the unrelenting heat of our house and his inability to take the steps to make himself more comfortable. Another was that he had become used to a routine at school and felt confused and lost when he didn't have it anymore—a common situation for autistic children. Another—the remote beginnings of adolescence and aggressiveness—was terrible to contemplate. Would that mean he'd simply get harder to handle as the birthdays passed?

We were now armed with Risperdal, the strong drug that had given the hospital staff a measure of control over him, and we felt reasonably confident that if another episode occurred, we could handle it. We now had a psychiatrist, but she regarded Walker's autism as a problem of control, a matter of figuring out the right dosage of Risperdal to keep the peace.

Life was better. With Davy now in third grade, Ellen and I were looking forward to the first full year in which *both* boys would be in school. We would experience "free" time to try to make more money to dig out of the black hole of debt we were in. Ellen could take on more freelance writing jobs; I could teach more overtime classes.

This state, our version of bliss, lasted just six weeks. Then the other shoe fell.

THIRTEEN

Davy Crashes

"See that sign over there? I think it has some wet paint on it and I think some of the paint is in the air and I think I breathed some of it. Am I OK?"

Davy rattled off this question fast, as if it were one absurdly long word, while he and I hurtled along Belmont Avenue in a taxi on a brilliant October morning. He was staring out the open window, his reddish-blonde hair blowing in the breeze, and he had an expression of horror on his face as though he and he alone could see that gremlin on the airplane wing from "Twilight Zone" grinning at him from outside the taxi.

"Davy," I said as gently as I could, trying to muffle the alarm in my voice, "you couldn't possibly have breathed any paint particles from that sign. And it's a half block behind us now."

"Yeah, but if I did breathe them, am I OK?"

"Ha, ha! You're OK." I sort of tut-tutted this as I leaned over him and cranked up his window.

Short pause, then: "I think I breathed some fumes from that truck in front of us. Am I OK?"

"Davy, there's fumes from cars and trucks everywhere, but it's all in such small amounts that no one gets sick. Don't worry about it."

"But the fumes are toxic. Am I OK?"

"Yes, Davy. You're OK."

The Middle Eastern driver turned around to look at us. He'd been hearing this "Am I OK?—You're OK" exchange over and over for the last fifteen minutes, ever since he picked us up from Davy's school. What was this, some kind of wacky American jive talk?

"Dave's having a bad day," I said.

An hour before this I'd gotten a call from the school: could I pick him up and take him home? Davy thought he was poisoned because he had breathed air tainted by the paint on a flagpole in the school playground. Ellen was out with the car, so I took a cab.

This was on Monday. The previous Friday Ellen had picked him up because he was convinced that he'd eaten a tiny piece of crayon in art class and that the crayon was going to kill him—"in six months." For a half hour, other kids ate pieces of crayon; the teacher ate a small chunk of it, swallowing hard and theatrically; there was a small crayon-eating feast, yet no one could budge Davy from his doomsday idea.

In the car on the way home with Ellen he was inconsolable and for the whole weekend he basically lay on the living room couch and sobbed.

After Davy and I got home, the questions—averaging about one every two or three minutes—didn't stop.

"Mom, you washed that floor with Mr. Clean and I think some of it came through the air and I think I swallowed some. Am I OK?"

"You're OK, Davy."

"Dad, I think the paint on that wall has some lead in it and some of it flew through the air and came in my mouth. Am I OK?"

"You're OK."

We quickly learned that no amount of reasoning with him helped. Common sense explanations—such as that he had more to fear from a dirty floor than the cleaner or that no paint in the house contained lead—were just miserable little infuriating exercises. He waited until he heard the magical words, "You're OK;" then he'd be quiet for a moment until the next toxic attack had to be fended off.

The following morning he rose and gave the day his usual greeting—"I'll rise, but I won't shine!"

So far, so good, we thought.

Davy ate breakfast while watching "Sonic the Hedgehog" on TV and marched happily off with Ellen to the car.

I saw Walker off on his bus, read the newspaper, took a shower, and while getting dressed, I heard the tramp of not one but two sets of feet on the back stairs. Davy trudged in, his face smeared with tears, dropped his anvil of a backpack on the floor and threw himself face down on the living room couch.

Ellen strained, relentlessly, for the silver lining: "He's too scared to walk into the school building. He's still worried about that flagpole. But it'll be OK, right Davy? You just need a mental health day to relax."

"Sure, Dave. It'll be fine," I told him and sat down on the couch at his feet. "Everybody gets nervous about things sometimes."

Ellen and I stared at each other with our well-honed, forced good cheer but had the same thought: "My God. Not Davy too!"

The days that followed were shattering for everybody. Each morning we went through a ritual that got progressively nastier as the weeks went by. At first, Ellen and Davy would drive to school, park the car, walk to the door, and then—body trembling, tears streaming down his face, screaming and tugging on Ellen's hand—he'd refuse to go in. Ellen would stand at the entrance and try to keep a stiff upper lip through the classic "skin-off experience"—mothers and children staring at them while Davy cried about toxic paint and crayons. Then, after a few days, he wouldn't get out of the car at all.

Inevitably came the stage when he wouldn't get out of bed.

Ellen and I discovered an interesting fact of parenting: getting a reluctant child to go to school is ultimately based on nothing more than bluster and bluff. When push comes to shove, short of actually pushing and shoving the child through the door, a parent cannot *make* a child go to school. What could we do? Catapult him through the door? Strap him into a harness and chain him to a desk? No punishment worked, no taking away of privileges, no screaming, no spanking, no threats. Nothing at all.

ELLEN AND I both knew the name for Davy's problem—OCD, obsessive-compulsive disorder. Ellen had had a touch of the trouble herself in graduate school and had done a feature article on it for a magazine. I had had a textbook case of it in the early '80s. At its height I would do something like this:

With no time to spare to get to class in the morning, I'd dash out of my shabby 3rd floor bachelor apartment, walk rapidly a block down the sidewalk toward the El, and a thought—one I'd identify as coming from Satan himself—would pop into my head: had I turned off the stove?

I knew that if I could get safely onto the train, with no turning back, like Ichabod Crane getting over the covered bridge, I'd be out of trouble and could put the thought behind me. So the mental dialogue began as I picked up my pace:

Now, Bob, this is nonsense. You know you didn't use the stove this morning.

Yes, but what if I used it last night and forgot to turn it off? What if the whole building burns down and mothers and babies with it?

Ha, ha, Bob! You know you checked the stove three times this morning. The damn thing is off, off, off! You know it!

Yes, but I can't really remember. I mean I can't *visualize* actually having checked it three times this morning. Maybe the checking I remember doing was yesterday's checking.

But Bob, you can't go back now. There's no time. It would be crazy, just crazy. You don't want to be crazy, do you?

So I'm late for class. What's that compared to the responsibility of saving the mothers and babies?

Then, a block from the El station, I'd curse myself, turn around, and hurry back to my building, fly up the stairs, dash into the kitchen where of course, as I knew all along, the stove was off, cold as a corpse.

I spent about three or four months being racked by crazy stray thoughts like this—the obsessions—followed by the compulsion component, the sensation of being involuntarily propelled back to the apartment. I had the feeling many OCD victims have, of living a secret parallel life, one in which I was pummeled by involuntary thoughts (Did I lock my office door? Did I tell the class about the test next week?), all the while doing a fair impression of normality in the presence of friends, family, colleagues, students.

I tunneled my way out of this mental prison by monitoring myself and giving myself little speeches: *So, Bob, let's say you did leave the stove on and the building does burn down with the mothers and babies inside, and the lives of many people are ruined, including yours. SO WHAT?!! WHO GIVES A DAMN?!!*

Soothed by that comforting thought, I'd stride purposefully to the El station, get on the train, and never think about the stove again. This strategy worked so well that the trouble virtually disappeared.

Until Davy.

What puzzled Ellen, me, Davy's psychologist and his psychiatrist, was the sudden onset of Davy's OCD and its severity. In all my months of private struggle with the problem, I'd never let it seriously interfere with my outward life: I never missed a day of work; I never looked especially distracted or upset. I had gotten over it.

But Davy's OCD was so severe his life had come to a halt. One day he was going to school, doing rather well; the next he was terrified of imaginary toxic dangers, too afraid to leave the house.

IN OUR ENDLESS discussions of the sobbing boy on the couch, we began to search our memories for omens of Davy's big crash. We began to see certain episodes in a new light.

There were unsettling, but in-the-range-of-the-normal episodes. He'd sometimes refuse to leave stores until we either bought some bright plastic gizmo for him or I performed my "carrying of the squealing pig through the door" routine. Or he'd insist, after getting strapped into the back seat of the car and we had just pulled out of the garage, that Ellen or I go back into the house to retrieve particular stuffed animals or particular blankets for him to hold for safety.

But only the Tree-Hugger Episode of two years earlier seemed to have the voltage of the emergency we were in.

On a wintry Saturday the four of us were leaving Indian Boundary Park, a big beautiful place on the far North Side with tennis courts, trees, a pond, a small zoo, and the ubiquitous wooden castle playground. We'd just spent two pleasant hours there and were about to cross the street to the car when we noticed Davy lagging behind. He was plastered to a huge tree, arms and legs wrapped around one side of it, cheek against the bark.

"Hey, Davy, come on!" I said. "Let's go get some ice cream."

"I'm gonna climb this tree. I'm not going 'til I climb this tree."

"But Davy," Ellen laughed, "you can't climb up. It's too big around. The nearest branch is way up there."

"No! I have to climb! I'm going up. Boost me up, Dad!"

I picked him up and held him against the tree. "See, Davy. The branches are too high. You'll never get up there."

He was screaming now. "It's not fair. I never get to climb trees! I'm not leaving 'till I reach the top!"

"Let's go climb that one over there," Ellen said, pointing to a low-slung, smaller specimen.

Davy remained plastered against the tree like a Pacific Islander caught in a hurricane. Walker started to yank on Ellen's hand and shout "Car! Car! Car!"

We pleaded with Davy, reasoned, threatened, joked, but nothing worked. Ellen took Walker, who was jumping, yelling, pushing, and tugging, over to the car.

After more useless talk, I peeled him off the tree, tucked him under my arm, and stomped out of the park. Twenty minutes later, eating some kind of pineapple sherbet swirl, Davy had completely forgotten the temporary madness that had come over him.

Nothing "toxic" in the episode, nothing school-related, but in its essentials it was the same phenomenon as we now confronted: an immobilized, despairing, and frightened boy locked onto an irrational thought.

IT SEEMED THAT, as with Walker, we were once again in the dark land of complete medical helplessness. Davy's psychiatrist, Margery Johnson, tried Luvox, then Zoloft, drugs that normally do a good job of helping kids with Davy's combination of depression and OCD. Neither worked. Rich Arend, Davy's therapist and best friend, suggested many techniques for the three of us to use, all of which we tried when we weren't panicked and shouting at each other, but behavioral strategies seemed puny up against whatever it was that Davy was facing.

Then one day Dr. Johnson phoned Ellen with a new idea. At a medical conference she had heard of a study being done at the National Institutes of Health in Bethesda, Maryland, on "sudden onset pediatric OCD." The researchers were looking for kids with "PANDAS" (pediatric autoimmune disorder associated with streptococcus). Their theory was that strep could cause the immune system to misfire and send antibodies into the brain, cause swelling in the basal ganglia, and thus actually trigger OCD symptoms. When the blood is cleaned, the antibodies are washed away, the swelling goes down, and the child is cured.

"Let's get a strep test for Davy," she told Ellen.

"But Davy doesn't have strep. He had it a few weeks ago, but he doesn't anymore. He's fine," Ellen said.

"Let's do it anyway," said Dr. Johnson. "Sometimes kids seem free of strep but actually still carry it."

Sure enough, Davy tested positive for strep, was a by-the-numbers example of a child with PANDAS, and the people at NIH were eager to see him. So Ellen and Davy were off, at government expense, for the experimental treatment.

ONE EVENING IN January Ellen called from Bethesda.

"Doesn't it seem in a way like Walker has OCD, too?" Ellen was saying.

"Could you wait a minute?" I said, and put the phone down. I stepped over to the TV set, picked up the remote, and paused Walker's tape of "Cinderella." "You've got to stop rewinding this scene, Walker, or I'll throw the tape away!"

"No stop today! Rewind! Rewind!" he shouted and tried to yank the remote control out of my hand.

"No rewind today!" I shouted back in Walkerese. "You've seen the damn mice put together Cinderella's damn dress about eight times now. You have to let the movie play through! Got it?"

"Got it," he said, trying to push me aside so he could see the TV screen. "I got it today."

Picking up the phone again, I said, "I'm sorry. He's driving me nuts."

"That's what I mean, the rewinding. Isn't that OCD behavior? Doing something over and over to try to control an out of control world—just like Davy?"

"I don't know," I said. "Davy is so different from Walker, so *normal.*"

Then Ellen said, "I know what you mean. Anyway it's just a thought."

Later that night, as we did almost every night, Walker and I got into the Bedtime Battle of the Kitchen Light. The battle always went like this:

At about nine p.m. Ellen and I would move the dining room table to the side a few feet, put a foam mattress and blankets and pillow on the floor, and Walker would fall asleep on his back with his face turned up toward the overhead light shining right into his eyes. He had a comfortable nest in the quiet bedroom he shared with Davy, but he insisted on sleeping in the dining room, and more: the TV, only ten feet away, *had* to be on; the door to the back room at the end of the hallway *had* to be closed; and the kitchen light, separated from the dining room only by a low partition, had to be on. He would have preferred sleeping in the O'Hare United Airlines terminal at Christmastime, but this was the best we could do.

That night, as usual, I graded papers and watched Letterman as Walker fell asleep. Then, as usual, I got ready for bed, opened the hallway door for the cats to reach the litterbox in the back room, and turned off the TV set and kitchen light. I left the overhead dining room light on, for a certain minimum wattage had to penetrate his eyelids to maintain REMs. But leaving the kitchen light on was for me intolerable. This bright light not only illuminated the kitchen and dining room, but our upstairs loft bedroom as well. I had a sleep specification of my own—darkness—and this was where I took my stand.

I was falling asleep at about midnight when I heard Walker shout "Light!" This was the traditional first shot in our nightly war games. Before I could react, he sprang to his feet, turned on the kitchen light, dashed down the hall, slammed the door shut, and leaped back into bed. All this was the signal for me, like a Confederate Civil War re-enactor, to go through the motions of resistance but lose the battle once again: go downstairs, turn off the light, talk sternly to him, (more often, yell at him) and hope against all previous experience that he would give up.

But tonight a light bulb, as it were, went on over my head. Frozen in the corpse-laid-out-for-a-wake position, I stayed in bed and thought, Maybe Ellen is right. All this stuff does look like OCD, doesn't it?

Take this stupid light. He's as vigilant about having it on all night as Davy is about dodging imaginary toxins in the air. It's as though both of them have little danger-detecting barometers in their heads: the slightest shift in the atmosphere in the room, the minutest alteration in what must remain rigidly the same, sets off all the alarms. Walker knows when the hall door has been left open, even when he's engrossed in watching a videotape, even when he's asleep. Davy *knows* when you've used Comet in the bathroom to clean the sink, even when he's in the living room drawing a cartoon.

Take the rewinding. Why does he do it? The professionals we've talked to don't even find this question interesting. Doctors especially seem highly uninterested in questions for which they have no quick answers. Psychologists call it "perseverant behavior" or "self-stimulation," and go on to suggest usually futile ways to stop it. Naming something seems to wrap it up for them, shut down questioning.

But these terms, I thought, don't explain anything. They're always thrown out in a patronizing way, as though the psychologist—who's never lived a day in our house and who, if forced to endure such agony, would talk about it ever afterward as a professional milestone—knows something Ellen and I don't. The term "self-stimulation," with its vaguely sick, masturbatory connotations, especially steams us. Jargon only pushes the problem away, makes the rewinding seem to be just another inexplicable, repellent ritual of an alien tribe, like cannibalism or voodoo.

But *why* does Walker do it? Is he trying to make sure he heard something right? Is he trying to understand a scene in hopes repetition would make it coalesce into something intelligible? Does he already understand the scene and is enjoying something he has finally figured out? Is he trying to communicate with Ellen and me by irritating us into reacting—the "Look at me!" phenomenon?

Or is it, as I now wondered, a straightforward obsessive-compulsive moment, with some of the above possibilities folded into it? He convinces himself, against all common sense, even against his own judgment, that the universe will fall to pieces if he doesn't check again.

I lay in bed staring up at the reflection of the kitchen in the skylight and thought about an agonizing moment on our last trip to Lincoln Park Zoo. Two days earlier, on a cold, dark, wintry afternoon, we were literally skipping past the habitat of the black bear and were

Walker, age 8, in Lincoln Park

happy to have the zoo almost completely to ourselves—actually a rather frequent situation for us. As I galumphed along next to Walker, I glanced at the bear who was busy doing what bears do best, banging on a large metal plate attached to a cliff-like wall. About to make the same tired observation to Walker that I always made at this point—"Look, Mr. Bear is doing it again! In the wild he wouldn't be caught dead doing anything so dumb"—I noticed that Walker wasn't skipping beside me. I wheeled around to see him running fast in the opposite direction.

I shouted, "Stop!" but he kept going until he reached a bend in the railing that marked a change in animal habitat. I ran up to him and said as brightly as I could, "OK, let's keep moving, man!" He zoomed off again, but this time he stopped short of the black bear and spun around so fast that I again sailed along a few feet without him. I stopped and watched him run back to the same point at the railing, then turn around. He looked very upset and anxious. He was frowning, jumping up and down in place, and crying "Ah! Ah! Ah!" I jogged over to him and said, less brightly, "We've got to keep moving, *now*. It's getting late."

We repeated this ritual in an ever-shrinking route until he was ricocheting back and forth about ten feet between two points on the railing. The sky turned from orange to black; the zoo grew very dark; Bang! Bang! Bang! went the bear on his metal plate. Not for the first time in the last few years I pictured the white truck I saw in a cartoon once—no, a dozen times—careening toward the two of us, its wheels barely touching the ground, and two men in white coats tumbling out of it, grabbing Daffy Duck, throwing him in, and driving away. How awful, yet somehow—*peaceful*. I threatened Walker, pushed him, and shouted at him. Nothing worked.

As I yanked on his hand to try to break the spell he was under, two joggers, a twentysomething man and woman, passed and scowled at us, the woman turning around to give the "What the heck is going on here?" look. Come on, come on! I thought. Say something! Come on! I had about six Snappy Comebacks in my mind's hard drive, not one of which I'd ever uttered. I had always dreamed of laying a sidewalk critic flat with one of them but always found myself too upset for clever repartee when trouble actually arrived.

With the zoo closing in five minutes, I grabbed Walker from behind, pinned his arms to his sides, picked him up kicking and screaming, and staggered with him out of the Force Field or Zone of Doom or Path of Peril or whatever it was he'd created for himself. Once through the gate of the zoo, he came out of it as though at the snap of a hypnotist's fingers, and was once again the happy boy he was before he'd entered the zoo.

My recovery was not so swift. I remembered the advice of a young hippie/prophet (or was he a paranoid/schizophrenic?) who used to walk slowly through the campus when I was in graduate school in the seventies. He'd repeatedly shout, "TAKE A DEEP BREATH! [long pause] AND THINK ABOUT WHAT YOU HAVE TO DO NEXT!" It seemed like a good idea now.

The night of the Battle of the Kitchen Light, I lay awake a long time just working over all this in my head and savoring the discovery: maybe Walker's autism and Davy's, Ellen's, and my OCD were all related. Maybe they were different versions or different degrees of the same thing. And if Davy's treatment at NIH works, maybe that or some other variant of the treatment would help Walker.

And the treatment actually did work! Everything about his case precisely matched the theory: Davy inherited a tendency to OCD from Ellen and me. Undetected strep caused a misfiring of his autoimmune system. Antibodies mistakenly invaded his brain and caused a swelling, and the swelling caused his behavior. When his blood was cleaned out in a procedure called plasmapharesis, the antibodies and swelling disappeared, and so did the behavior.

Presto! No more OCD.

In the days before his long and nauseating plasmapharesis, he was going up to random people at the hospital and asking, "Excuse me. Do you have AIDS? I'm afraid of AIDS." And then in a stage whisper to Ellen: "I think I breathed near that guy and maybe I breathed some AIDS germs. Am I OK?" Then Ellen had to apologize to the person (who quite possibly *did* have AIDS since there was a research study going on in the same wing of the hospital) and lurch ahead with Davy to the next awkward moment. But two days after the treatment Ellen phoned me sounding happier than I'd ever heard her.

That morning she and Davy had been on the elevator with a man in a wheelchair. He was emaciated and seemed to be at death's door. He gripped an IV pole and was leaning over and vomiting into a bucket. Davy stepped over to him, patted him tenderly on the shoulder, and said, "It's OK. I know just how you feel. I had plasmapharesis two days ago and I was throwing up on the elevator too. But you'll be OK."

My God, we thought. What if there were some magic wand for Walker too?

FOURTEEN

Liftoff?

Our new suspicion of an autism–OCD link made us feel like scientific superstars. We had that Copernican–Einsteinian *Ah-ha!* sensation of realizing we had been looking at the picture upside down all along: Autism was a *medical* problem, not a so-called *behavioral* one. The fact that as we dug further into the question and found that others, many others, had made this discovery before us hardly dampened our satisfaction. We had a new quest.

By the 1980s when Walker was born, doctors and therapists had progressed beyond the behavioral "refrigerator mother" idea that somehow autism resulted from a child's shrinking away from a stiff, unloving parent. They knew autism had to have some medical or genetic basis. But they continued to approach the problem behaviorally anyway. Escape from the condition, if it ever came, would be through clever conditioning and teaching. Medical science was the source of medications to control the child, help to make life livable, but it wasn't the source for a cure. The rule *Autism is incurable* had the spurious force of the old rule that *Nothing can go faster than the speed of sound.*

The experts therefore sent a mixed message to mothers: you didn't cause the problem, but you're not equipped to fix it either. You need to turn your child over to professionals like us who can give him "the services he needs."

Maureen, our most trusted expert and Walker's best friend, had hit a wall with him. Never flagging in her enthusiasm, never doubting for a moment the presence of a real boy behind the screen, and never failing to come up with new creative approaches to teaching him, she nevertheless was baffled by the slowness of his progress. At eleven, after three years of therapy, he had improved in a way that gave us heart: he was using more words in longer statements and even the increased shouting was a good thing, a sign of his strong desire to verbalize. But his progress was glacial. The language gap with other kids his age was now so immense we wouldn't have dared tried to calculate it in the developmental way of "Johnny is six but speaks at a the four-year-old level." Maureen was essential, PACTT school was essential, Ellen and I were essential, but we needed more.

Since Davy's treatment at NIH, we had begun to believe that doctors existed who actually listened and kept an open mind, who did not radiate hopelessness, who tried things that might help.

Davy's psychologist, Rich Arend, told us about a pediatric neurologist, Dr. Michael Chez, in Lake Forest, just an hour north of Chicago, who was doing research studies based on the same suspicions about OCD and autism that we had. If this kind of research proved successful, Rich joked, it could someday eliminate a lot of therapy with pills and treatments and "Put me out of a job."

We called to make an appointment with Dr. Chez. The first opening the doctor had was in five months because parents from all over the world—medical geniuses like ourselves—were seeking him out.

IN THE INTERIM before our appointment, we had a visit to a doctor that illustrated where general pediatric knowledge of autism was, c. 1997. It was an ordinary doctor visit for Walker—to check out a possible sore throat—but it was the sort of thing that only pressed on us the urgency of getting past conventional medical attitudes.

Walker reacted to strep tests as he would to torture by the Spanish Inquisition. Weirdly enough, when he had a shot or blood test, he would sit calmly and stare curiously at what the nurse was doing with the needle, but the harmless say-ah routine threw him into convulsive fits of self-defense.

After only two minutes of struggle to get his mouth open, we were already working with Nurse Number Two. We were hopeful, though—we could tell this one meant business. I crouched behind Walker, pinning his arms to the back of his chair. Ellen kneeled at his feet, holding his ankles together. The nurse—called in by defeated Nurse Number One—gripped his chin with her left hand, positioned her body almost on top of his, and in her right hand held her tiny stick just out of sight. She was grinning like she'd never had so much fun in her life. Cool and in command, she waited her chance. Walker shut his jaws tight and squirmed with all his might.

We reassured him like happy torturers.

Ellen: "Oh, Walker, you're doing a great job!"

Nurse: "What a brave boy you are! And so good-looking!"

I strained to get into the spirit but failed: "This is so *stupid*. You've done this many times before. You know it doesn't hurt."

Suddenly Walker shouted "No doctors today!" I rolled my eyes. The nurse pulled back in triumph and said, "Got it! Good job, Walker! I'm so proud of you!"

Brimming with admiration of her, I thought *So far, so terrific*. The last time we had taken Walker for a strep test, we went home frustrated because the nurse was unable to reach the back of his throat. Of course, as far as we knew, Walker didn't even have a sore throat this time. Since he never told us when he felt sick and wouldn't answer our questions, we had to infer illness from his behavior: irritability, angry shouting, increased compulsiveness.

The three of us then waited in the examining room for the result of the test and the consultation with the doctor. Waiting with Walker was never easy. He would start out patiently enough, for he was always curious about his surroundings and eager to see his pediatrician, whom he liked. But if he had to wait very long, at some point he would just explode, shouting and jumping. When the exam was finished, Ellen would go to the desk and pay the bill while I rushed Walker past a waiting room full of goggle-eyed parents eager to check us out.

This day, to head off his restlessness, Ellen and I were joking around with him. Since he was devoted to songs and had a great memory for their lyrics, we could always break him up by doing new, extemporaneous rewrites, no matter how achingly dumb ("Home, home in the *car*/ Where Daddy drives real *far*...") Then the doctor knocked and came in. Unfortunately, it wasn't our regular pediatrician, who was out of the office that day. It was a doctor we never saw before, a handsome, white-haired, slightly bent old gentleman wearing a beautiful white shirt and blue tie and a happy, relaxed, reassuring expression on his face. He smiled benignly and said, "Hello, young man."

Instantly Walker leaped up and shouted "Car! Car! Car!" and brushed past the doctor toward the door. Taken by surprise, the doctor put his hand over his tie and stepped back. While I leaned against the door to keep Walker in, the doctor raised his voice enough to be heard and reported that Walker's test was negative and that he probably just had a virus.

Then, pulling himself together and benignly beaming once again, he said, "You know, he's a big strong boy. He's only going to get bigger and stronger. Have you thought about that? What's your plan?"

What's our plan...? Ellen and I didn't dare look at each other, for we knew we had the identical thought: *Yikes! We never thought of that. We'll get right on that, Doc.*

Getting home forty-five minutes later, we huddled in the back room with Walker out of earshot and in the dining room. We exchanged the "plans" we had been working on silently in the car.

"Doctor," Ellen said, "We thought we would pray to win the LOTTO. Then, after we get a hundred million on my birthday because it's my good luck day, we'll use the money to buy ourselves a *real* doctor who would think night and day about curing Walker instead of predicting hell for his future."

"Oh," I said, "but I thought our plan was to feed Walker raw meat and eggs and pump him up with steroids and get him to lift weights until he was the size of Arnold Schwarzenegger and then train him as a hit man to wipe out our enemies."

We went on in this vein for a while and really let the poor doctor have it. He had assumed that the future—our most obsessive worry night and day for years—was something we couldn't possibly have contemplated. More than that, he seemed to have momentarily mistaken himself for a veterinarian discussing the fate of a pit bull or Doberman. *After all,* he seemed to think, *a boy like this couldn't possibly understand what I'm talking about.* He was also, we thought, put off by our upbeat attitude itself: *This kid is a disaster. Why are these people smiling?* Pediatricians had just one thought about autism—it was incurable—and therefore child rearing was a question of management, containment.

OUR CONTINUING HOPE for a cure could seem nutty to a pediatrician or any outside observer. But from our point of view our persistence didn't seem strange at all. The boy himself was always presenting us with small vivid reminders of how near the Regular Kid actually was.

One afternoon that previous summer when Davy was off at his day camp in Evanston (we tried to give Davy as much normal life as possible), I took Walker for a drive and just kept on driving and driving. We were listening to *The Hobbit* (we now had a later-model Escort with air-conditioning and a tape player) and we both were feeling fine. He sat next to me leaning his head against the window and looking down and smiling in the Intent Listener Position. I too was mentally with Bilbo Baggins in the dark woods and before I knew it, we found ourselves in Wisconsin.

We were near Lake Geneva, the site of many pleasant family vacations when I was a kid, and I decided to share with him my memories from the golden days of yesteryear. We stopped off at Yerkes Observatory, a beautiful Victorian edifice that had represented to me as a kid the romance and adventure of my future life as a world-famous scientist. We got out of the car, and with Walker holding my hand and leaping up and down, I took him for a "walk" on the grounds. I told him how one late summer night in the '50s I had looked through a telescope parked on the golf course next to this observatory and peered at a comet. The telescope belonged to a friend of my father's, a tall thin man named Mr. Petersen who smoked a pipe, and I listened eagerly to his little lecture on what a comet was and how lucky we were to actually see one.

But this day, in 1997, bouncing along next to me and tugging me back to the car, Walker showed no more interest in the story of my astronomical moment than he did in the sight of the giant, strange-looking domed building.

Undaunted, I drove Walker over to the nearby George Williams College Camp, where my family had spent many one-week summer vacations during the Eisenhower administration.

"I LOVED THE smell of DDT in the evening," I was saying to Walker after we'd parked the car. "A big truck would come right down this hill here and spray a smelly cloud of stuff in the air to kill the mosquitoes."

When in my determined, not-lazy gear, I didn't worry about what he could understand or not understand; I just rattled on like a compulsive monologist. I hoped that he secretly understood it all. I knew that he understood a little of what I said. And I was certain that he was alive to the emotion behind the words. I pressed on: "I could hear the truck way off in the darkness getting louder and louder. I liked to pretend it was an enemy tank coming to get me. I'd hide behind the wall of the tent where the bad guys in the tank couldn't see me and as it passed a cloud would come into the tent. Boy, that was fun!" Then I looked at him.

Even a normal ten-year-old boy would grow restless listening to this gripping trip down memory lane, but Walker seemed to be repelling it with his entire body. Walking along next to me, his left hand in mine, he managed to angle his left shoulder up to his ear and plant his right index finger in his other ear. If not for the big grin on his face, he'd look like a refugee trying to block the sound of artillery fire.

So I laid off the soliloquy for a moment and just remembered. College Camp was the anti-matter inverse of the Levittown-ish suburb where I lived. Oak Lawn was flat; College Camp was hilly. Oak Lawn had tiny new trees (no oaks); College Camp had towering old ones. Oak Lawn had not a single feature of geographical interest; College Camp had the big, clear, blue lake. Our tent was perched on a wooden platform a few feet above the ground. It had no electrical connection and was lighted by a single oil lamp on a table. The buildings at the camp were late Victorian frame structures with vast porches. You could sit on them in big wicker chairs, play cards, gaze at the sparkling lake and feel the breeze through the trees. We ate in a large refectory where we were served by cool college students, and chocolate milk could be had at every meal.

This was *living.*

Walker jerked on my hand and I snapped out of dreamland. "Let's go over to the ice cream parlor," I said. "I used to come here every night with Aunt Pat, Uncle Larry, and Uncle Pete," I added, thrillingly.

Inside at a small round table, Walker sat in an almost relaxed position (though his shoulder never left his ear for very long) and devoured a cup of vanilla smothered in chocolate sauce.

When we stepped out and I looked down the road, I was hit by another nostalgia attack.

"You know, Walker, every time I left this place to go back to our tent, I ran down this hill. Boy, I was just crazy about running down this hill."

Just at that moment he grinned, looked up at me, and tore off down the slope yelling "Ah-ah-ah-ah-ah-ah!"

For once, instead of chasing after him, I just watched him go, skipping and running freely with his arms raised, laughing and shouting all the way down and up the rise in the road a short way. He suddenly stopped, turned around, and smiled back at me.

It was a small thing, a very small thing, but it was very nice. It was enough to keep me thinking that maybe medical science could do something to help pull this boy out into the social world.

A VIDEO OF our first appointment with Dr. Chez would play like a Three Stooges short: three adults shouting to be heard over the yelling of a big eleven-year-old boy; the tall, bald father wrestling with the kid while trying to talk, peeling the boy's fingers off the doorknob and throwing his arms and legs over him; the attractive mother nervously smiling and shouting the boy's medical history, trying to absorb what the doctor is saying while monitoring husband and son; both parents, when they can be heard, using words like "intelligent" and "cooperative" and "friendly" to describe the wild kid jumping hysterically in place, tearing at the door and pulling on his father's hand; the friendly, energetic doctor strangely calm while trying to examine the boy who is yelling "*Da da ees pareez!*" and "*No Donald's today!*" into the doctor's face; and the overall impression of pandemonium—if the scene isn't intended as farce, it must be tragedy.

The video, however, would not reveal what this meeting in fact was: *one of the high points of our lives.*

Dr. Chez not only agreed with our theory of a relationship between OCD and autism, he was way ahead of us on it. He had studied it, written papers on it, had done groundbreaking NIH research himself. He was familiar with all the procedures Davy had gone through and talked to Ellen as one insider to another. He wanted to know everything we had been thinking and theorizing about Walker, all of our unscientific, nonempirical, agonizingly minute observations. Far from being turned off by our enthusiasm about our son, he welcomed it. Far from thinking of Walker as hopeless, he saw possibilities in him.

In the middle of the raucous interview, I offered to take Walker out to the car so Ellen and he could talk. "Oh, no," said Dr. Chez loudly and brightly. "I'm learning a lot from just watching him right now. Everything you're telling me about him fits what I'm seeing."

It does?! we thought.

He was especially interested in Walker's big seizure six years earlier. He asked us if they had taken an EEG. Yes, we told him. Had they done a *sleep* EEG? No, we said, the neurologist at the hospital told us he was far too wild and restless to fall asleep and keep electrodes on his head all night. Dr. Chez said that we'd have to get a sleep EEG before we could do anything else. We looked at him doubtfully.

"We can do it," he told us, and he explained that a child can have seizures throughout the night, unknown to the parents, and the medication can be altered to prevent this from happening.

"How does he sleep now?" he asked.

"About as badly as humanly possible," we shouted, or words to that effect.

While we were walking out the door of the office, he smiled and said, "I think we're going to see big improvement, and soon."

As we drove home on the expressway, we felt elated, as though the seatbelts we wore were the only things keeping us from floating around weightless inside the car. Here was a doctor who spoke to us like we were grownups...who took us seriously...who didn't see us as the Duke and Duchess of Denial...who thought Walker was as interesting as we did...and most of all, who held out hope that Walker could get better and wasn't afraid of looking like a chump if he didn't. It was that—the typical doctor's fear of being wrong, the insistence on worst case scenarios both to lower expectations and to appear wise—which was especially galling to us about the medical profession and the Developmental Police in general. Like Maureen, like Laurie, Dr. Chez was willing to predict success, however foolish the prediction might appear down the road.

MY FATHER, WHO had worked for Illinois Bell Telephone Company all his life (as did his father before him), used to say that the company hired only women to be phone operators because women were much more patient with the nonsense customers threw at them than men would be. Even when I was a kid, I wondered if my dad was relating a psychological fact about the sexes or simply generalizing from what he knew about his own short-temperedness. In my case, I knew I didn't have a particle of the patience of a phone operator. In any stressful situation dealing with other human beings, there was no question about it: Ellen was the one for the job. This was why Ellen went with Davy to Bethesda, staying up all night with him during the grueling plasmaphoresis procedure. This was why Ellen was the ambassador to the world of experts. And this was why she *had* to be the one to stay up all night with Walker in the hospital for his EEG.

So Ellen was by his side as he struggled to get out of bed, rewound videotapes and audiotapes, sat up bouncing and waving his arms in the signal we had come to know so well—left arm straight out to the side, right arm raised at a diagonal on the other side, roughly semaphoring the letter 'Y'—and shouted "Daddy!" "Home!" "Car!" and "No hospital today!" over and over. He threw up the medication they'd used to help him relax and get to sleep. Through it all Ellen stayed by his side, kept him in the bed, explained to him endlessly why he was there, made friends with all the nurses, pretended all was well. She was determined to make this work.

And it did work. Around four o'clock he fell asleep for a couple of hours. The machine detected that yes, he was having seizures in his sleep, and Dr. Chez switched his medication from Tegretol, which the previous neurologist had prescribed, to Valproic Acid. He told us that we might not see any results for a few weeks. "Results," we knew, would mean Walker sleeping through the night.

DR. CHEZ HAD breathed new life into our hopes for Walker, but he could do nothing for another problem that we became increasingly aware of. "Don't you guys ever get *out?*" was the way the issue was always put to us by friends. "Yes, but do you make time for *yourselves?*" was a typical response to our daily Boy Report.

Never getting out didn't seem like much of a problem to us. Does the staff of an emergency room pause in the middle of an influx of bus crash victims and ask, "Yes, but are we making enough time for *our-*

selves?" Besides, we were on a mission. We were zealots with a feverish ideology: *The children come first.*

We had no aversion to babysitters, as such. But we knew enough about Walker to fear anybody's attempts to deal with the craziness he could throw at them. Would Walker stick his head in the toilet, as he had once done when we visited a friend's house? Would he poop in the corner of our bedroom? Would he bite the babysitter out of frustration over not being able to communicate something his parents normally picked up by telepathy? Would he shake the babysitter the way he did his Grandpa Jack once, gripping Jack's hands so tightly and jumping up and down so wildly I had to step in and pry the two of them apart? Would he get out of the house and run away? Would he shout and thunder through the house slamming the front, then the back door? Would he break more furniture? Walker had so far—out of excitement, never out of malice—broken four couches, two armchairs, two beds, two end tables, one dining room table, and about thirty trampolines. Finally, would he get sick and not be able to let the babysitter know?

Thus from about 1987 until October 1996, Ellen and I never had a date. And we seldom visited others as a family. The notable trip to Peter and Anne's house when we discovered trampolining was a rare exception. We'd seen our friends Tom and Christine in Indiana a few times, but Walker's high-maintenance qualities always swamped our enjoyment. Even when he was quiet our minds were always on him: *What is he doing? What will he do next? How will we manage him when he does it?*

To see us friends had to come to our house; the mountain—the four of us—couldn't, wouldn't, come to Mohammed. We lost touch with some people; for only the most dedicated would put up with this system. We knew it had to be done this way, but it was impossible to relate this convincingly to anyone.

We were like perpetual shut-ins who had forgotten what fresh air was like.

NOT LONG AFTER Ellen's adventure with Walker in the hospital, I had a conversation that reminded me of the need to open a window once in a while and breathe some oxygen. I was standing by the faculty mailboxes in the English Department at my school, and I decided to regale a couple of colleagues with one of my better Walker stories.

It was a regular war horse—I thought of it as "The Fatal Case of Beer"—and I knew that Ethel and Alan, two people with strong sense-of-humor credentials, would recognize it for the knee-slapping laugh riot I knew it to be.

I told them how one sunny Saturday afternoon Ellen and I found ourselves *actually relaxing and watching* a film on TV, a delightful monsters-created-by-atomic-testing movie from the fifties. I was feeling smug, I explained, because Davy was quietly playing a video game upstairs and Walker was silently on the computer in the back porch room. I related how, at a commercial break, Ellen went back to check on Walker and as she opened the door felt a cold drop of *something* fall on the back of her hand. She looked up and another drop fell in her eye, and another on her forehead. Then she realized that the entire ceiling was covered with droplets of beer dripping on everything in the room: the computer, the printer, books, stacks of paper, laundry.

I described the scene: how Walker stood grinning and dancing in place in the middle of the room surrounded by exploded cans of Budweiser, another carbonated grenade in his hand, ready to shake, pop open, and decorate the room once more; how Ellen took the can out of his hand, turned around, slowly shut the door, and walked slowly back into the living room with a strange smile on her face; how she walked up to her husband stretched out on the couch like a comfortable corpse—a corpse with a can of beer in his hand—and deadpanned, "Robert, you might want to check out the party Walker has been having. It's very... *interesting.*"

I then paused and looked at their faces like a stand-up comedian waiting for the gales of laughter—*that did not come!* Instead they looked grave and nodded sympathetically. "Oh, it must be so difficult," Ethel said. "Don't you two ever get out?"

Deep in my child cultist heart, I knew it: Ellen and I *did* need to get out.

Ellen found a "respite service," a private organization that hires people to come to a house and watch over handicapped children or bedridden family members who need constant care so that the stressed-out relatives can escape the house for a few hours—all this at no charge to the family.

They sent over someone they said was "experienced": Cathy, a Native American, a self-described "cowboys-and-Indians Indian," a young woman with a big smile who radiated warmth and calm. Her full-time job was caring for men at a home for disabled adults, and she told us she was used to just about anything. *We'll see about that,* I thought.

Thus it came to pass that on a lovely Friday summer night, Ellen and I found ourselves giving Cathy babysitting instructions with all the urgency of dying pilots telling the stewardess how to land the aircraft. Then we reluctantly left the house and walked to the Biograph Theater to see a movie, our first date in ten years. Until this night we had always seen films in shifts: one of us would go, then the other, and the rule was we couldn't discuss it until we had both seen it. Sometimes, as with the movie "Bull Durham" (Ellen went one night and I the next afternoon) this worked so well and we both enjoyed it so much that we had the illusion of having seen it together. Most other times there would be such a long time gap between each other's viewing that there would be no "date" feeling about it at all.

So this was a huge event, the couple-that-never-appeared-as-a -couple out in public at the same time, and it was awkward. When we got to street corners, I'd throw my arm out like a crossing guard in front of Ellen, holding her back while I scanned the traffic for an opening. Strolling along, I'd keep ahead of her just a bit to watch for cars, dogs, and bicycles. When we got to the theater and to the narrow alley where John Dillinger was shot in the 1930s, I blocked Ellen again with my arm, and she said, "What, are we dodging bullets now?"

We got to the theater a bit early, so we crossed Lincoln Avenue (safely!) and sat in a coffee shop sipping cappuccinos the way we imagined normal people did. It was a strange feeling, sitting across from one's spouse trying to avoid Topic A all the while obsessing about it and wondering when the beeper will go off that will call us back to the scene of a disaster that surely no stranger, no matter how "experienced," could possibly handle. I tried to make conversation with Ellen but rarely made eye contact, my eyes busy staring into the middle distance at the scene at home in our living room: Walker flinging himself about and screaming, Cathy weeping in the kitchen and frantically looking for the beeper number, Davy hiding under his bed for protection.

During the film, though the beeper never went off, Ellen and I yo-yoed from our seats to the phone in the lobby for updates on child mayhem and each time heard Cathy's high, musical voice saying, "Oh, the boys are just fine. No problem at all." *Was she shielding us from the truth?*

When we got home—surprise!—the house was still standing, and the boys—bigger surprise!—had smiles on their faces. Davy had made a new friend, had plied Cathy with questions about Indian life ("Really, Dave?" I found myself saying to him when I walked in the door, "Cathy's actually eaten bear meat?") and Walker seemed delighted to have met someone new, someone who talked to him as if he were a real person who had real feelings. They had made popcorn. They had listened to bluegrass music. They had watched "Animal Planet" on TV.

And we had found a babysitter.

IT WAS ELEVEN p.m. a couple of weeks later. We'd just gotten back from Date Number Two, a more relaxing experience this time, and we'd just gotten Walker ready for bed. We'd pulled out the dining room table and dragged out the foam mattress from the back room. We'd laid out his blanket and pillow and turned on the light overhead. We'd kissed him and said good night. Then we witnessed a genuine, flat-out medical miracle. He said, quite distinctly, "Bed now." He carried his pillow and dragged his blanket down the hall to his bedroom door. He walked in, turned on the light, walked around the bed of his sleeping brother, went over to his own bed, lay down and said, "Light!"

Ellen and I were standing at the doorway, speechless. I turned off the bedroom light and closed the door.

"OK. What just happened here?" I whispered to Ellen in the hall.

"Could it be the medication?" Ellen said.

IT *WAS* THE medication. Every night thereafter Walker would say "bed now" and off he'd go into his dark room and contentedly sleep through the night without waking. Sleep—regular, consistent, blessed sleep—was had by all for the first time in eleven years. Ellen, trying to imagine what it meant to Walker, said he couldn't have *liked* sleeping out in the dining room with the TV blaring, lights on, his parents talking. But somehow he thought it was safe. She compared Walker's mental state to that of a Londoner during the blitz. It wasn't pleasant to sleep in the underground, but it was secure. The medication must have turned off the alarms in his head and given him the all clear. Night held no terrors for him now.

Besides joy, we also felt a kind of rage. This simple development—a neurologist prescribing the right medication so Walker wouldn't have continuous night-time seizures—should have occurred years ago, at the time of his first big epileptic emergency. We had thought, as his previous neurologist assured us, that since no dramatic, life-threatening seizures had recurred, that there was no seizure activity. But there *had* been, over and over, every night, and now no one could tell whether or how much brain damage had occurred over the years. This neurologist, a kindly woman who encouraged us to think positively, had a fine reputation. And the North Side Chicago hospital where we had taken Walker when he stopped breathing on that horrible long-ago night had a far greater reputation than small Lake Forest Hospital where Dr. Chez worked and where Walker had had his EEG.

All those years of exhaustion and bad parenting and guilt and worry in the middle of the night—all of it was unnecessary! All of it could have been averted! We had taken the word of experts that Walker's wakefulness and shouting in the night was just "another one of those things autistics do," a behavioral problem to be fixed with some Skinnerian magic. But it was a medical problem with a medical solution.

Late one night when the boys were asleep in their bedroom and the TV was off, Ellen and I mulled over all this by the fire.

"You know," I said. "We could sue the hospital over that misdiagnosis. Look at all that misery we went through."

Ellen was standing with her back to the fireplace, her arms at her side and palms turned backward to catch the full heat of the flames. She was smiling and shaking her head. "I don't think so. For the first time, we have a solid piece of medical progress and a good doctor who wants to explore new ideas. I don't want to look back. We're moving forward."

I looked at her doubtfully.

"Look," she said, "Walker's in school, Davy's in school, we even have a babysitter. And I'm starting to get more work."

She moved her hands around in front of her and rubbed them together. "We have liftoff."

FIFTEEN

Apocalypse, Again

I was standing in a gym and nervously holding Walker's hand as he jumped in place. I kept thinking *Where are the counselors? They're supposed to be here by now. Walker's timer is about to go off. These people are supposed to know: autistic children can't wait.*

It was 9 o'clock on a June morning of 1998. The "liftoff" of over a year ago had been real enough, but it was more of a pokey, Wright brothers-style, low-flying experience than the jet-propelled flight we were hoping for. Davy's OCD had returned, not in the intensity that had caused him to miss school, but enough to cause trouble for all of us. His condition was triggered by viruses, and the viruses couldn't always be kept at bay. Walker was sleeping through the night, and that was very good, but adolescence was upon him and he was harder to handle. Now twelve and a lean, muscular 5'10", he required ever more attention.

My eyes were locked on the entrance to the gym. *Where are the damn counselors?*

Ellen had paved the way for this moment as best she could. She had met with Trevor, the head of the program, a week earlier and phoned him again the night before. He was accommodating but odd. He had a nervous manner and seldom looked into your eyes. He spoke in a loud, abrupt, commanding tone of voice like that of a boot camp officer. And he insisted his name be pronounced "Tree-vore." It was this last trait, waved like a flag of idiosyncrasy on meeting him, which should have tipped us off about the trouble to come.

Ellen explained that Walker had a severe problem and that his version of "first day jitters" could be very, very bad if he had to wait. So it was important that when he arrived, his aid would be there, ready to receive him and talk him through the new experience. (Walker was the only child in this group of largely autistic children who required a personal aid.) The whole summer, she cautioned, could be ruined by a traumatic first day.

Trevor pooh-poohed her fears. "I'm sure it won't be any problem, Mrs. Hughes. Your son will have a good experience here. I know just what to expect from these kids."

But here we were, at precisely nine a.m., and no counselor of any kind was in sight. "Where are the grown-ups?" I said to one of the children in the near-empty gym.

"I don't know," the little girl said. "I guess they'll be out of there some time."

"Out of where?" I asked. But she disappeared.

Then Walker started to yell: "HOME! HOME! CAR! GO HOME!" He was not at the kicking and biting stage yet, but I knew that he'd given up on the uncertainty of anticipation and crossed over to snug certainty of rejection. He was having none of this.

As more children arrived and Walker's restlessness rose, I launched into my usual routines of trying to control him, complete with surface amiability and subsurface panic. The key was to prevent his impatience from spilling over into anger. Moments like this always put me in mind of the old "Incredible Hulk" TV show when Dr. David Banner would warn a bad guy, "You don't want to make me angry. You wouldn't like me when I'm angry." If Walker "lost it," the scene he made could be very bad.

Fifteen minutes went by. No counselors in sight. Twenty minutes, then twenty-three minutes went by, and we were on our way back out to the car. We were through the doors when a booming voice called to us from behind. "Hey, Walker! Aren't you staying?" It was Trevor in a bright blue T-shirt and carrying a styrofoam cup of coffee. He was sauntering—the relaxed developmental professional reassuring a nervous parent—and had a female blue-shirted counselor at his side.

We came back, hand in hand, and Walker tried to pull himself together. Agitated but making an effort, he looked down as Trevor introduced Sarah, who put her arm around Walker and spoke gently to him. "I'll be with you this summer, Walker. We're going to have lots of fun."

"He's in pretty bad shape," I whispered to Trevor. "We've been waiting for half an hour."

"Oh, don't worry, Mr. Hughes," he bellowed and I jerked my head back. "He'll calm down...WON'T YOU, WALKER?"

Walker just looked down at the ground.

So I left him there, chalking up any misgivings I had to overprotectiveness. *You've got to trust people more, Bob,* I lectured myself. *Walker's got to get out more on his own.*

WHEN I WALKED in the back door a half hour later, Ellen asked, "Well, how did it go?" Just as I was about to answer, the telephone rang. She picked it up, said "Hello," and said nothing for a couple of minutes. Then: "OK, we'll be right there."

"We have to go back to the park. Trevor says Walker took a bite out of his counselor's arm and he had to take her to the hospital."

"My God, is she OK?" I asked.

"He wouldn't say. He just said Walker 'took a bite out of her arm,' whatever that means."

As Ellen and I hopped into the car and sped over to the park, we imagined Sarah in shock and her arm gushing blood and the end of Walker's participation in the program, possibly in any program. When we got there, Trevor was shaking his head and holding up three fingers.

"We can't tolerate biting here," he said. He lowered one finger. "Two more incidents like this and he's out of the program."

(Always, always in incidents like this, a silent accusation comes through: biting or kicking or screaming or spitting or pulling down one's pants may be encouraged in your family, but it is not what we do here.)

"How is Sarah? Was she bleeding badly?" Ellen asked.

"She'll probably be OK."

"Will she need stitches?"

"Uh, I don't think so. No skin broken. No bleeding."

What? No bleeding? What are we talking about? We both suspected something we'd seen before: Trevor was "building a case" against a difficult kid he didn't want to have to deal with. (Later that night Sarah called us and explained that Trevor had made her go to the emergency room, that she'd wanted to stay, that the incident was nothing to her really, and that she was more concerned about Walker's fear than anything else.)

Trevor said we should take Walker home and return the next day for a "trial period."

ON THE WAY home, the three of us pulled into the McDonald's across from Wrigley Field as the crowd was swarming into the park. We paused in the Drive-Thru lane as the stream of fans eddied around us. It was a brilliantly sunny day for a ball game, the early part of the great summer slugfest between Sammy Sosa of the Cubs and Mark McGwire of the Cardinals. Everywhere there were families trekking from their cars to the gate.

One group in particular caught my eye. Five blonde children, two of them as young as four or five, walked blithely in front of the car—inches in front—followed by their mother, a pleasant-looking blonde carrying ballpark supplies. "She's not even holding any of their hands!" I said, amazed. "She knows they can walk safely in a busy parking lot! We can't even take Walker to a Cubs game, much less let him stroll through a parking lot like this! I can't even remember the last time I tried to bring him here. He wouldn't sit still for even a minute..." I ground on and on like this for a while—one of my talents.

Ellen just stared straight ahead. We watched this happy group passing on the other side of the windshield as if they were sea creatures in an aquarium—Normals in Natural Habitat.

As Walker shouted "Fries!" over and over in the back seat, I felt the near presence of an old enemy, self-pity. At moments like this I usually fought him off by reminding myself that even the Normals had personal troubles that made them feel like real life was happening somewhere "out there" being led by "other people."

But I hated them anyway, hated them all.

ELLEN TRIUMPHED OVER Trevor. Through persuasion, friendliness, and flattery laced with veiled suggestions of possible litigation, she managed to keep Walker at the camp with an aid for the summer.

But something was up. There was a restlessness and agitation about Walker that we couldn't define. In some ways, he was doing better. He had a school he liked now, he continued to have a great relationship with Maureen, Dr. Chez (whom Walker adored) had embarked on a new program of medication that seemed to have some good effects, but that summer we found we had to watch him more carefully than ever.

Walker, of course, was always a very watched boy. His every action fell into unwritten, unspoken but very real categories in our minds:

Action Type A: Good for us/Good for him: Mysterious brief solar flares of complex sentences and normal play and personal preference—and, much more commonly, his day-to-day good cheer and emotional connectedness—that kept us hopeful about his potential.

Action Type B: Good for us/Bad for him: Repetitive, zoned-out behavior like rewinding of videos or audiotapes that kept him quiet and out of our hair so we could get work done but reinforced bad habits.

Action Type C: Bad for us/Good for him: Pooping in our bedroom, urinating at the front door, shouting unintelligible requests in our faces, and other obvious attempts to communicate and break through barriers that were nevertheless very, very hard to take.

Action Type D: Bad for us/Bad for him: "Psychotic episodes" and other nuclear blasts of despair.

It was this last category that applied to the situation we found ourselves in late on a Sunday morning in August. Davy and I had just returned from the supermarket to this scene: An end-table smashed in the living room; Ellen upstairs on the bed crying; Walker jumping up and down on our bed with a wild look in his eyes and shouting "NO THIS TODAY!" Walker, Ellen explained over the shouting, was in the middle of a total cataclysm, a full-bore episode—a fact I could confirm immediately because I had to dodge a tape player that came flying near my head. While Davy and I had been shopping, Walker had broken a coffee table, thrown a Coke across the living room, torn through the house pounding and shouting, and had tried, again and again, to bite, squeeze, and push Ellen. Every day that summer we had seen brief demos of this behavior, but not since his first "episode" had we seen this particular look in his eyes and this particular determination to stay over the top. Now he was taller, heavier, and stronger than before, and used his new powers to freeze his family into a rigid state of alert.

As Davy tried to carry on with normal life, Ellen and I discussed the meaning of Walker's behavior while wrestling with him, screaming at him, threatening him, and watching him. We gave him an extra milligram of Risperdal, the drug we had been giving him since the last episode to control just this sort of behavior. But it had no effect. We called the doctor and got permission to give him an extra dose of Adderall, his Ritalin-like drug, but this had no effect either. His detonations continued with great frequency until, at eight p.m., with Davy having given up on normal and under his bed with a book and a flashlight, we admitted defeat and took him to the emergency room.

The hospital Intro was, of course, awful. The big strong twelve-year-old thrashing around on the floor of the emergency room...the staff unable to budge him so that I had to drag him into an examining room...Ellen alone with him for three hours in the small room with nobody even checking on them...our boy so wild when entering the psych ward that Ellen doubted the staff could handle him…the two of us throbbing with despair about him through it all.

But it was the Exit that was the real killer. After five days, on the day before he was discharged, we met with the psychiatrist on staff. He spoke to us in such kind and gentle tones, with such quiet tact and sensitivity, that it took a while to realize that he was reading us the riot act.

"Well, Walker has improved enough to be discharged tomorrow, but I'm concerned about what will happen when he gets home. Except for the few hours when he was sleeping, we've had to have at least three nurses near him at all times. I wonder how you will be able to manage," he said and paused, looking into our eyes across a table in a conference room.

It was the old implied message: you people are up to your eyeballs in Denial. Will you just stop and look at this kid? But this time our own alarm matched his.

"The trouble is, there is no next step after he leaves. There's no hospital situation other than this one, and this is prohibitively expensive," he went on. "You should look into a [very tentatively now]…residential home…of some kind because it looks like he'll need something of the sort before too long. Unfortunately I have no specific information for you on where to look."

The residential home idea, as much as I feared it as a possibility in the future, was not my main concern just then. I was focused on the next day and how I was going to get him the twenty feet down the hallway of the ward, onto the elevator and out the door and into the car without help from some kind of hospital SWAT team. Each day when we visited him, Walker showed only slight improvement. He was as restless and anxious to leave on Day Five as he was on Day One. And this time, two years after his first Apocalypse, he was stronger, heavier, and a couple of inches taller. How would I keep him from attacking me long enough to give an impression of control? How would I even get him into the car if his Car Intro mania took hold?

The next day at eleven a.m. Walker and I stood at the big locked door to the psychiatric unit ready to leave. I smiled nervously, shook everybody's hand, and thanked the nurses who stared doubtfully while Walker jumped in place, pulled on my shirt and shouted "HOME! HOME! HOME!" without let-up. The scene was so different from when we brought him home after he was born. The nurses then were funny and reassuring and confidence-boosting. Today there were no encouraging words, just curious silence, as if they, like me, wondered how we'd get down the elevator and out onto the street. But we did get outdoors and we did drive away.

As I drove, he adjusted his position continuously, putting his hands on each side of the seat and boosting himself up as though on parallel bars. Then he'd let himself down slowly. When his rear touched the seat again, he boosted up and repeated the process. He did this again and again, as if inaccurate placement meant the space capsule would fly out of orbit. He shouted one-word demands at me—"FRIES!" "POPCORN!"—because parents can magically make these things appear at will. I took him for a long ride punctuated by frequent stops at the side of the street to lecture him about being quiet and sitting still. I told myself we'd re-establish our peaceful riding in the car routine this way, but in truth, I was afraid to take him home. What would he do when we walked into the house? Would he snap right back into his psychotic episode state? Judging by the wild look on his face, this seemed entirely possible.

Whatever sense of security we had, pre-episode, had been pulverized. In the days and months ahead, he settled down a great deal, went to school and fell into his old reassuring daily patterns, but he had a new, ever-present potential for explosiveness. Because we were never sure of what he might do next, we went into a mode of too-obsessive vigilance. It was easy now to imagine an outburst turning into a rampage, a rampage swelling into an emotional tsunami. So I became even more than ever like his big shadow. The loose, sad division of duties from before (Ellen was Davy's parent, I was Walker's) tightened up. Walker's size and aggressiveness made it less feasible for Ellen to try to control him. I didn't dare go out on expeditions with Davy anymore for fear Walker would do something. In the house I was seldom more than ten feet away from him—steadying him, responding to trouble, policing him. The post-Apocalypse II lifestyle was very tense and exhausting and riddled with anxiety. Was it the way life was going to be? Would it just get grimmer and grimmer?

IN THE LINCOLNWOOD Town Center Mall six months later, the four of us are sitting in the food court on a Saturday afternoon eating hot dogs at two separate tables. Davy has insisted on being with me, so Ellen and Walker are together two tables away. I of course am keeping one eye on Walker.

The food court is the sort of place I never would have stepped into years before when I was a would-be-hip single person. I would have sneered at it as an environment that was garish, sterile, anaesthetic, and infra-dig. But I love the place now. It's loud and busy and few diners notice or care if a boy shouts, spills a Coke, waves his arms in a sema-phore shake while staring excitedly up at the rafters where small birds nest, or works himself into an open-mouthed, wide-eyed state that makes him resemble the subject in a nightclub hypnosis act. I enjoy sitting here chatting with Davy or talking unilaterally with Walker while looking over the banister at the shoppers and kiosks on the floor

Davy at 1½, Walker at 4 in Tennessee at Thanksgiving

below. We're out of the house, we're in the world, and we're having fun.

Suddenly Davy pops me with a question that hits me like a blast from a shotgun: "Dad, why don't you and Mom get a divorce?"

"What, Davy? Why would we do that? Mom and I love each other."

"Well, if you and Walker lived somewhere else, then Walker wouldn't yell at night and I could, you know, do my homework, and sleep. I could live with Mom and you could visit me and take me places on the weekend."

This, coming from Davy, is truly dire stuff, no mere idle idea. He's thought it through and obviously has had good reason, with his family under such pressure, to come to this conclusion. In the past he has always shown heroic patience with his brother. He has perpetually tried to empathize with Walker and even act as ombudsman and interpreter for him. Ellen and I have gone around and around about the effect on Davy of having to live with a brother like Walker. We usually conclude (rationalize?) that of the two, Davy certainly nets more attention from us because it is only natural to focus more on the boy who can barrage us with words—questions, jokes, requests, observations, arguments.

So I tell him to count his blessings, while all the time imagining the comebacks he is too polite to hit me with. I explain that I know it's very rough to live with Walker, but many kids aren't lucky enough to have parents who are happy with each other. *Oh, good for you two!* That many kids have a big brother who hates them and picks on them. *My brother doesn't hate me. How wonderful!* That though Walker's much bigger and stronger, he never hurts you. *Or killed me. Oh, thank you thank you thank you, Walker!* That some Dads are seldom home. *You're not always such a treat when you are around, Dad.* Or who have big fights with their wives. *Right. You haven't killed Mom yet. What a guy!* Or who have a drinking problem. *But what about the gallons of coffee you drink and the stress you contribute by being so hyper?*

I tell him all these things while it breaks my heart to see how much responsibility he's taken on. An incessant creator of worlds himself, he's just trying to engineer a solution to the fix he finds his family in.

I realize too, the more I think about it, that his solution is propelled by empathy. After all, he doesn't want to see Walker alone and living in an institution—the very idea is horrifying to him. No, he imagines a solution in which he himself would have a little more normality in his life but each of them would still have a parent.

Not long afterward the four of us go out to the parking lot and pile into our tiny car. As we drive away, I point out to Ellen a slight grey-haired woman standing with her son—or perhaps it is her grandson—on the sidewalk. The boy is strapped to a large board that stands nearly upright and has wheels at its base, a kind of dolly for humans. Clearly, the boy has some sort of spinal injury or muscle disease and a trip like this to the mall must require mountaineering-level planning on the woman's part.

I say to Ellen, "You know, whenever you think you have it bad, there's always some family that has it worse."

"Yeah," Ellen says, smiling, "but you had to reach pretty far for that one."

I had to agree. I'd done enough reaching for one day.

IT HAD BEEN a good day. It was 8:30 on a Friday evening in the early spring, and Ellen and I were relaxing and watching a movie on TV. True, there had been that nasty business at the footbridge out by Lake Michigan earlier in the afternoon, but that was just a blip on the day's clear radar screen, I thought.

It had been a sunny afternoon, the first warm Saturday of the spring, and the sidewalk autobahn-by-the-lake was in full throttle. Runners, bikers, rollerbladers, speed-walkers, and skateboarders had turned the relaxing North Avenue Beach where Walker and I ran virtually alone all winter and spring into an orthopedic surgeon's dream. An endless torrent of speeding bikers tried to avoid collisions with sidewalk- hogging rollerbladers; runners looked over their shoulders to see if bikes would sheer off a leg if they veered around slower, older joggers. The only small bit of sanity in the melee was the highway rule: keep to the right and you just may stay alive.

But Walker had to keep to the *left*, just as he had all winter.

Therein lay the rub.

We were running in the grass well off to the left side of the human highway, when I realized with a twinge of horror what we were approaching up ahead: an extremely narrow pedestrian walkway over a boat channel right alongside Lake Shore Drive. The bridge would be filled with people moving in opposite directions single file as fast they could, bumping elbows as they went. Surely Walker, the boy with aerial photographs of Chicago imprinted on his brain, knew what was coming too.

So I spoke to him. "Now, Walker, when we get to the bridge, you will have to run on the right. There's just too big a crowd today. You have to stay on the right. It will be just a short distance, and then we can go back to running in the grass."

He smiled and said nothing, but I knew what the Prince of Obsessive-Compulsiveness would say to me if he could just as certainly as if he had the voice and diction of James Earl Jones.

Now, Dad. You know *I have to cross the bridge on the left side. I have to I have to I have to. If I don't, my entire sense of ontological security will vanish; the world as I know it will explode into tiny fragments; there will be nothing left but waste and void, to say nothing of the darkness covering the abyss. Don't try to stop me!*

So there we were, the two of us trapped on a raft on the rapids of OCD, about to collide with a wall of humanity.

The crossing was everything I thought it would be, and worse. Shocked faces. Frequent collisions. Great confusion. Muttered obscenities. Near smash-ups. Shouted warnings. All of it caused by a man wrestling with a tall thirteen-year-old boy who was kicking and fighting to position himself in front of the oncoming traffic.

But this was OK. It was just a few moments and then, fifteen minutes later, I had recovered, and we were fine again, running together, smiling, taking in the scene. I teased him with silly lyrics to familiar songs and he laughed like I was a great comic. He turned in unexpected directions and led the way to explore new territory.

Viewed with the widest possible lense, this was a good outing.

That evening as Ellen and I sat watching "Bringing Up Baby," I convinced myself that I was feeling fine. Various components of Bob's Good Mood were in place: a great movie; Davy in the back room chatting with friends on the Internet; Walker bouncing on his big therapy ball (a longer-lasting, more economical alternative to the trampolines) in the dining room behind us. Setting him up had taken some time, but he was now successfully multitasking: bouncing, eating spaghetti, listening to Alan Jackson on his tape player, and laughing occasionally at scenes in the movie.

Suddenly he started shouting a phrase that sounded like "da da eece pareece" over and over. We had heard these words before but had never been able to decipher them. I paused the movie and went over to him and tried to spell it out on a piece of paper for him. But as I wrote down the letters, he put his mouth against my ear and yelled: "DA DA EECE PAREECE!!"

Then, amazed at myself, I watched what I was doing as if I were a character in a video: I threw the pencil at the wall, crumpled up the sheet of paper and yelled as loud as I could: "SHUT UP YOU DAMN KID! SHUT UP…JUST SHUT THE FUCK UP!" He shrank back away from me and I slammed my fist on the shaky table. Then I shook the sore fist in his face. "STOP IT! GODDAMN IT. STOP IT!"

"Walk away, Robert!" Ellen shouted at me. "Just walk away."

I stormed down the hall and out the back door. I went into the dark garage and started yelling obscenities. I picked up our rusty, seldom-used garden rake and smashed it against the brick wall, breaking the wooden handle and sending the metal rake end flying onto the hood of the car. I picked up a big bag of wild bird seed and…

[But perhaps it would be best to draw a veil over what the Hulk, Sr. did in the garage that evening and rejoin him later when the children are asleep and he is discussing child-rearing techniques with his wife.]

Ellen the diplomat reminded me that "we" usually lost patience with Walker when "we" were most anxious about him and secretly despairing. But, she pointed out, when he tries hardest is often the most difficult time for us. We'd been living through months of extreme stress with his yelling, but it was "good" yelling. [Vide Action Type C, above.]

"He shouts because he just wants to be a person in the room like we are. He's trying to push the words out any way he can. We always think we're staring at him so closely and looking at things from his point of view, but we're never doing it with as much attention as we think we are. We don't know exactly what 'Da da eece pareece' means but we do know that at least he's saying 'Pay attention to me, Mom and Dad.'" (She didn't remind me that he probably wasn't saying "Terrorize me please, Dad.")

"If we keep in mind what he's really doing, he'll still be really irritating," she went on, "but we won't feel so crazy. He's a teenager, and he needs to rebel but can't smart off to us. It's bound to make him nuts, like he has tape over his mouth. Maureen, his teachers, his aid at camp all say he's improving. We just have to hang in there for him."

So we decided to take stock of where Walker was at age thirteen:

- He was talking in longer sentences, many of them hard to understand but definitely meaningful, and he was getting through "intros and exits" more smoothly, waiting more patiently.

- He was yelling "Maureen!" a great deal between sessions with her, a fact which we took to mean that he craved the intelligent, confident attention and educational pushing of his oldest friend, as opposed to our impatience.

- He was watching videos less and watching regular TV with us more, even insisting at times that it be turned off entirely.

- He was getting taller—he was now an even six feet—and handsomer as an adolescent and was vain about it, had a more knowing look in his eyes and an even greater than usual eagerness to share "in" jokes with us.

- He was continuing to be a vigorous, athletic boy who keenly enjoyed his world.

We even patted ourselves on the back: our one indisputable accomplishment was that we had kept the smile on his face, the smile we were so impressed with when we called him "Little Ronald Reagan" as a baby.

We never, ever in our late-night pow-wows exchanged an inventory of his *in*abilities—this we did privately and reflexively all the time. He was so far from the competence and worldliness of a normal thirteen-year-old that putting our thoughts into words would only have dragged us down. But he was, emotionally at least, very much the normal teenager: or rather, we thought, a *better*-than-normal teenager.

I went to bed that night not a new man, not an improved father, not any less guilt-ridden. But I did see Walker and myself a little better, and that was something. It was enough, anyway, to fall asleep and face another day.

SIXTEEN

Hope

I was telling Ellen that evening about something I had read on an autism website. It was one of those healthy, positive comparisons that are meant to buck up the spirits of parents with disabled children. It said that discovering your child is autistic is like taking a flight bound for Hawaii and, upon disembarking, finding that you've arrived in Amsterdam by mistake. You're disappointed, of course: it's chilly and rainy and dark there. But, the story implied, if you have the right attitude, you find living in Amsterdam has its own unexpected joys.

Ellen looked at me like I was out of my mind. "Hey," she said, "I've been to Amsterdam. Amsterdam is wonderful. I know hell when I see it. *This* is hell."

I had to agree. Three months had gone by since the Hulk-in-the-garage episode, three months in which Walker seemed to shout and never stop. I suppose he did actually stop from time to time, but it never seemed like it, for we were either shell-shocked from the last blast or were trying to pull ourselves together for the next one. We'd give him time outs, and he'd cooperate and go to his room, but when he came out again he'd shout again.

He'd yell demands—"ICE CREAM!" "SPIRALS!"—or agendas—"PACTT SCHOOL THEN PARK!"—or seeming nonsense—"HOLIDAY INN!" "NO BUS TODAY!" He was taking plenty of medications meant to manage him—his pills plus Davy's OCD and allergy pills plus my own 49-year-old falling-apart-guy pills made our kitchen look like a small pharmacy. We'd evolved from our early anti-medication attitude to a belly-up-to-the-bar one. "Has Walker taken *all* his pills?" was a frequent question. "Unfortunately, he has," was the frequent, disappointing answer.

The routine each evening was this: He'd bounce on his ball and shout. One of us would walk over to him and talk to him. He'd quiet down for a minute, but when we walked away he'd start shouting again. He wouldn't write, draw, look at a book, sing a song. The household revolved around him. Davy did his homework in his bedroom or hid out in the back room on the computer. Ellen and I pretended to work or read or watch television, but we were really full-time attendants.

On this April evening Ellen walked down the hall a bit and signaled me to follow her. We went into the back room and shut the door.

"Davy and I were talking and we think it's a good idea," she said.

"What's a good idea?"

"What would you think about getting a puppy?"

I laughed. Then I stared at her. *This wasn't a joke!* "Why, I think that's a terrific idea!" I said. "Also…backpacking in the Andes! Playing the violin at Carnegie Hall! Flying my Lear jet to Cannes with my co-star Penelope Cruz! Yes! I'm having fun already."

So Ellen and Davy drove out the next weekend to the suburbs to buy a Shetland sheepdog puppy. Davy spotted one with a certain engaging–expectant look in the eyes. "I like this one," he said. "This puppy looks optimistic. Can we call it 'Optimism'? They discussed it for a while and decided on "Hope."

Ellen's solution to this long disease, our life, was to pour *more* life into the house. She'd already taken in four cats from the alley. "Maybe Walker will like Hope. She's a darling puppy. And shelties are supposed to be very good with children," she said when they brought the dog home. Shelties are also known in the show-dog world as "talkative" animals, i.e. they bark forever.

But it turned out to be a fine thing. Walker was amused by Hope; she was always trying to "herd" him in one direction or another. Wherever Walker went in the house, Hope was at his feet, nosing him and blocking him. We even got used to a new pleasant sound: Walker giggling at the little dog underfoot. Davy too had an adoring friend who followed him outside when he rollerskated or skateboarded. And Ellen and I were distracted by her and were forced to focus less on Walker and what he was or wasn't doing. We took her out for walks and got to know other dog owners and neighbors we had never spoken to. We had a new identity: we were Doggy People conversant with Doggy Issues.

IN RETROSPECT, HOPE'S presence was a sign of how, in the spring of 2000, life began—almost imperceptibly—to ease up for us a little.

Several things—all of them Action Type C—happened around that time to indicate that Walker was changing. One was the Paula incident.

Paula was Walker's new aid at the city park special recreation group where Walker went after school. Tree-vore was now long gone and the people in charge there were very good—smart, spirited, and happy. The place now had an altogether better ethos.

But I was uncertain about Paula. She seemed ill at ease with Walker and slightly afraid of him. One day I got a call from her. Could I come and pick Walker up? He had said an obscene word and he needed to know he couldn't say things like that at the park.

"Really?" I said, very doubtful of the whole thing. "You must have misunderstood him. He doesn't go around saying obscene things." I thought the whole idea was very funny.

"Oh, he said it all right," Paula reassured me.

"What did he say?"

"I don't want to repeat it. It's not appropriate."

"Really now. You can tell me."

"Well, Mr. Hughes, he shouted 'suck it' over and over again."

When I got off the phone, I laughed and laughed. *My God*, I thought, *if he said that it would be a breakthrough! I'd slap him on the back and congratulate him! I'd pop open a bottle of champagne!* But I knew the truth. She misunderstood him.

When I got there to pick him up and realized that Paula was sincerely trying to teach Walker a lesson about his bad language, I got mad. I let her have it: "You just don't want to deal with him. He's not a boy who would even know what he was saying! I'm very disappointed. I thought you would know more about him by now."

She was upset but I didn't care. She needed to be taught a lesson.

Three weeks later Walker and I were at a table in the middle of a new cafeteria at Lincoln Park Zoo. As we ate our french fries and drank Coke, we observed the crowd of busy eaters all around. Bumping chairs with us were mothers and small children with extravagant Lincoln Navigator-type strollers equipped with everything but air conditioning and video screens. The place was like a playground for well-off moms and their tots.

Suddenly my tall thirteen-year-old shouts in my ear, "SUCK IT!" I looked down and thought *There's no mistaking it. That's what he said.*

I whispered to him, "OK, Walker. I think we're finished. We better get going."

"SUCK IT!" he shouted again.

I gathered together the backpack, his jacket, left our food on the table, and tried to maneuver him through the babies and supermoms.

"SUCK IT SUCK IT SUCK IT SUCK IT!" was what the young teenager said to the middle-aged man, holding hands with him as they tiptoed through the crowd and out into the air.

Once again, I thought, I'd underestimated him. If the boy were as normal as I kept telling people he was, of course he'd pick up on a term he'd heard at the rec group, a term that got a strong reaction from people. Like any teenage boy, he liked to shock—he'd certainly shocked me enough times. What better way was there for him to say, as he seemed to say every day at home: "Here I am! Pay attention to me!" The autistic "closed off, lost in a world of his own" kid was the most devilishly connected person in the room.

And I'd underestimated Paula too, and how thoughtfully she was trying to do her job. I knew I had some apologizing to do, but I was a seasoned pro at that.

Another lesson for me. And the lessons just kept coming and coming.

ANOTHER INDICATOR THAT Walker was doing better was the cat episode.

The only regular visitors to our house were Ellen's good friend, Teresa, and her daughter Franny, Davy's pal. Because they generally came over on a Friday or Saturday evening and stayed for several hours, they were able to witness some of Walker's more notable nonsense.

We'd order out from one of the dozens of ethnic restaurants within a few blocks' radius of the house and play board games, chat, or watch a movie. Walker felt very close to Teresa: he'd sit near her at the table, blush when she spoke to him, and try to speak to her from time to time. She had a pleasant, musical voice, and Walker, we knew, loved that quality in his women.

One Saturday night in May we were sitting around the table after a Mexican take-out dinner and were discussing the Clinton marriage. Davy was in the back room at the computer with Franny, and Walker was silent upstairs with his tape player on.

Suddenly we hear a shout from above: "TERESA!" We turned and looked up and saw Walker leaning over the upstairs banister holding Louis, our furriest, friendliest, most beloved cat, at arm's length over the edge. "CATCH THE CAT!"

"Walk-er..." I started to say, gently, like the western sheriff to the bad guy, "Just put down the gun. You don't really want to hurt anybody." He held Louis out a moment more and then—*flying cat! thud!*—Louis hit the floor and...*ran back up the stairs!*

We sat there, stunned for a few seconds, and then again "CATCH THE CAT!" and Louis flew and plummeted exactly as before.

This was no game to encourage, but it was one to take heart from.

THE MOST ADMIRABLE thing Walker did that spring was begin destroying videotapes.

On a Sunday afternoon, Walker was watching videos, Ellen was in the kitchen, and I was upstairs on the exercise bike. Suddenly we heard a sharp *crack* like breaking plastic. I stopped pedaling and looked over the edge. Walker had a videotape in his hand and had intentionally broken off the front, pulled out the tape, and was walking into the kitchen.

"What did you do?" Ellen said as he brushed past her. He then hurriedly stuffed the broken tape in the wastebasket under the counter. Ellen pulled it out. It was one of his favorites, "Cinderella."

"Walker, look what you've done!" she said. "You broke one of your favorite tapes. Well, we're certainly not going to buy another one."

Later when we tried to discuss what he'd done, we couldn't get anywhere. It was just too bizarre.

The next day during a rare moment when we were both out of the room, we heard the tell-tale *crack*. Then another and another. We dashed into the living room to see three tapes—a Disney sing-along, a "Thomas the Tank Engine," and Disney's "Donald in Mathmagic Land"—on the floor. He had another one in his hand.

Finally, it sank in: he was sick of his own compulsion to watch these tapes and was taking extreme action to release himself from it. *Good for you, Walker!* we thought. We took the hint. We gathered up all the tapes in the house, put them in bags and boxes, and put them in the basement. We put the VCR high on a closet shelf, and no one, not even I, watched a single video for the next four months.

SEPTEMBER 2000, A gray Saturday. The two of us were downtown at the northeast corner of South Water Street and Michigan, waiting for the "sign of the walking man" light to change and let us move ahead. Every time we crossed a street, I impressed on him the absolute rule that no walking could be done until we saw the man. Outside of Walker's getaway Fourth of July run down Addison Street years ago, he had never actually crossed an intersection alone, but I was prepar-

ing for the "future"—when? if? the time came when he'd be doing it
every day.

Bright Orange Hand changed to Striding Guy, but Walker didn't
move. "Write," he said.

"Huh? Let's go," I said and tugged on his hand.

"Write it down," he said, louder this time.

I sighed, stepped back with him away from the corner, and pulled
a spiral notebook and pen out of my backpack. (Contents: first aid kit,
telescoped umbrella, Walker sweatshirt, loose change, water bottle,
can of Coke, Walkman, baby wet wipes. These last were to clean his
hands, face, neck and ears from time to time because as he walked, he
dragged his fingers across the walls and windows, then put his fingers
in his ears when something or someone he saw was too exciting.)

"What do you want to write?" I asked him.

"Chicago River Water Tower Oak Street Beach," he said with no
pause between the words.

I thought for a few seconds. *He's reciting our route,* I realized with excitement.

I wrote the words down, tore off the sheet, gave it to him, and we proceeded north toward the river.

While we walked, he dragged the page across the display windows, the guardrail of the bridge, the statue of Jack Brickhouse until, by the time we reached the Water Tower, the sheet was torn to shreds. So we stopped and I wrote a new agenda: "Water Tower. Oak Street Beach. Zoo. Lions. Tigers. Monkeys. Flowers." It reminded me of the wonderful moments when, as a four- and five-year-old, he ran through the house with the short sentences I'd written on large pieces of paper, and of when, as a two-year-old, he'd go to bed with words he'd spelled in block letters. But never before had he demanded his agenda written out for him.

It had always frustrated everyone who worked with him that writing down a day's schedule in the morning didn't reassure him the way it did other autistic children. Autism seemed to create deep insecurity about a reliable course of events, as though it pushed the weather wonk's obsession—"morning showers diminishing by noon, high in the lower seventies, cooler near the lake"—to its outermost edge. One would think that a boy as interested in words as Walker was would love a morning list, but one would be wrong.

Maureen's efforts with conversation and writing had never stopped, however, and they were paying off. From that moment at Michigan and South Water Street, the lists multiplied. Everything had to be written down, traced with someone else's finger across the letters, repeated aloud. He wrote words with difficulty, sometimes with the letters superimposed on each other. But he also started picking out words on the computer keyboard again, and so an old laptop we had became his and rested beside him on the table at his station in the dining room where he ate, monitored which doors in the house were open and closed, played audiotapes, bounced on his therapy ball, watched TV, examined books, and now wrote words and sentences.

THE RESULT OF all these developments as Walker grew from 5'11"
at fourteen to 6'2" at fifteen—that is, the increased talking, humor,
writing, reading, needling in-your-face interaction, and the atten-
tion-getting stunts was a more relaxed boy and a happier house. Our
evenings, just when we thought we couldn't take the yelling anymore,
began to ease up and become bearable. Our fears of a bigger, stronger,
more aggressive Hulk, Jr. diminished. The shouting continued, sure
enough, but he cooperated better and showed an awareness of the
need, as a Very Big Kid, to take care not to alarm anybody.

Why the change? Some theories, developed in late-night conferences (television usually off):

(a) Walker was changing naturally, somehow "growing out" of his
earlier wild, confused state. Walker's form of autism fell near, but not
precisely on, what is called the Landau-Kleffner area of the spectrum
of autism disorders. Thus, it was possible, we hoped and prayed and
fantasized, that he'd just "get better." No medical expert would
strongly back this notion, however.

(b) Maureen's persistence, together with the environment at
PACTT School, were making a difference.

(c) Mom and Dad got off the dime and started writing with him
again and taking him more seriously again.

(d) Aricept. This is a medication that helps Alzheimer's patients
that Dr. Chez prescribed for Walker as part of a trial. It helped a good
number of children in his practice increase their language capacity, in
some cases dramatically. In Walker's case, though, the cause–effect
relationship of the drug and his improvement is possible but less
certain.

(e) The stress-lowering effects of Hope, the dog, and hope, the
emotion, the latter produced by the growing community of smart and
generous supporters of all types—doctors, nurses, therapists, teachers,
friends—lessening the burden and boosting our psyches.

(f) Walker's sheer determination, resilience, and happy nature.

(g) Some unknowable combination of the above.

OR WAS THERE one more factor—friendship?

Late one cold January afternoon I arrived early to pick up Walker at the gym where his after-school park program meets and Jose, the upbeat director of the group, told me Paula and Walker were outside taking a walk by the lake and weren't back yet. I walked out of the gym over to the lake and waited for them.

It's a beautiful spot. A big tree-filled park stretches in front of a broad beach with the infinite-seeming Lake Michigan a dark presence just beyond. This vast expanse of Nothing was always a surprise to me, having just come out of traffic where the scene is jammed with Everything. As often happens, I heard Walker before I saw him. Dimly in the distance I could make out two figures approaching on the sidewalk, one tall, one short. They briefly walked under a light and I saw Walker bouncing along on tiptoe, a big smile on his face, head tilted up, with Paula at his side.

When they reached me, Paula said, "Walker, why don't you go into the gym and get your backpack?"

"Get your backpack!" Walker repeated with energy, as if this were some great adventure.

Paula smiled and said, "Sorry. I guess I just lost track of time. Walker gets pretty upset sometimes in the gym with all the noise, and so we take long walks."

"Oh, no, don't be sorry," I said. "It's wonderful that you do this. Thanks." Paula and I had been friends ever since I made a fool of myself in the Great Suck It Caper.

"You know," she then said very hesitantly, "I think I get as much out of these walks as Walker does. He looks out at the lake or at the trees or snow and he seems to enjoy everything so much. It's like a…I don't know…like a privilege to be with him."

I looked at her, embarrassed to feel so thrilled. *She gets it*, I thought. *Somebody* else *gets it*.

June 2001

T his book has not told the story I sometimes dreamed of telling when Walker's autism first hit our family with all its force. The other story was a secret fantasy that ran through my head as I fell asleep at night. In it, a mother and father possessed of ultra love and ultra brains, together with fierce independence and persistence, found a cure not only for their own son but for all children with autism. This husband and wife, who looked sort of like Ellen and me and sort of like Susan Sarandon and Nick Nolte in the film "Lorenzo's Oil," had charisma to burn and selflessness like nobody's business. At the end of the book, Walker himself adds a postscript that inspires forever all the children and parents who find themselves up against a crippling disability.

Over the years this story receded from the repertoire of soothing scenarios that helped me fall asleep at night. (Pitching no-hitters at Wrigley Field, however, still works just fine.) Every other day or so some one thing would occur that made the story seem too far-fetched, even for a fantasy. Sometimes it was Walker's inability to say some simple thing despite constant coaching and coaxing. Sometimes it was my own unheroic anger flashing out at him in reaction to his shouting or spitting or refusal to try a new game or book. Sometimes I would glance at him and the contrast between his size (now six feet and growing) and his inabilities (at fifteen he still can't tie his shoes or point) slapped me in the face without warning.

But in place of the fantasy, a story with more solidity and reality gradually took hold. Ellen and I have both learned the lesson, to paraphrase Bette Davis, that hope is not for sissies. We've learned to accept—even expect—the electric shocks of disappointment as the necessary consequence of keeping hope aloft. We're able to do this because others are willing to do it too—willing, even, to risk looking like chumps when they fail.

I can be exhausted at the end of a weary week and growing gloom about him, and Maureen will emerge from their hour together with a sunny report about how he had initiated, in his own inimitable style of course, *a topic of conversation!* Ellen can pick up the phone on a dark afternoon and hear from an excited teacher at school that he has just *read almost a full page from a Harry Potter book!* All agree that he is improving. All agree that no one can set a limit to how far he can go. And all know him as a satisfying young man, one who has a small, encouraging surprise up his sleeve for a friend with a quick eye and an open mind.

AT THE SOUTH end of Lincoln Park on a brilliant Saturday afternoon, Walker and I sprint through a pedestrian tunnel and emerge behind the statue of Benjamin Franklin. Breaking with our normal routine, Walker sits down on a bench, and I'm happy to follow. Besides feeling tired, I'd like to take in the clear blue sky and the breeze. More and more lately, Walker gives himself a break and sits and watches. At fifteen, he no longer propels himself forward as though he thinks he can accelerate forever.

He sits with his left index finger in his left ear and looks down at the ground, occasionally looking up at a runner going by or at the dirty, wrinkled, and wet sheet of notepaper in his right hand. The sheet has on it our afternoon route and he has rubbed it against many surfaces, including some of the very things the words represent.

"Water Tower" has been mashed against the rough stone surface of the pumping station of the Water Tower itself. "Oak Street Beach" has made contact with the entertaining four-spigot drinking fountain there.

Ben Franklin has his back to us today. I often imagine that portly, pleasure-loving old Ben must look down from his high pedestal mystified at the exercise-crazed Americans swirling around him. His odd-looking presence here has always seemed to me like a fine excuse for a history lesson. I'm in the habit of telling Walker little things about Franklin, and we once read a children's book about him together years ago.

I'm thinking about this when darker thoughts seep in against my will. What does Walker really know about Benjamin Franklin? Isn't it likely that, instead of thinking of him as an inventor and Founding Father—the way I present him—he thinks of Franklin as a doofus with a silly voice who stole all his best ideas from a mouse—the way Disney, Inc. presents him in the video he's seen a million times?

I let this thought jerk me to the other thought that I fight off every day: how far Walker is from where we hoped he'd be by age fifteen. All the hard work with him, all the talking, all the tutoring, and here I am, still wondering what, if anything, he actually knows about Benjamin Franklin.

He snaps me out of my reverie: "Write!" he says, still holding the piece of paper in his right hand.

"What do you want to write, man?" I ask him, and pull out the notepad I now carry perpetually in my back pocket.

"I want please," he says. This is the introduction I must print to nearly everything now. If I don't, in some way known only to him, whatever I put down simply does not count. So I, his obedient secretary/interpreter/teacher/pal do as directed. I think I know the words that will come next: "ducks," "geese," "monkeys," "penguins"—the names of animals we will pass in the zoo up ahead. Instead, he dictates "swimming pool...Dr. Chez...Santa Claus Ho Ho Ho."

This new list takes me by surprise. As we read the words out loud together, I realize that this is not a current-reality schedule like the other one; it's a future agenda, a wish list. The first and last terms are obvious: a swimming pool is a place of ultimate fun—Walker loves the water and is a successful, fierce dog paddler; Santa Claus is, well…Santa Claus. But why Dr. Chez—a person he sees about twice a year for thirty minutes at a time? Then it hits me: Dr. Chez represents hope for Walker, an authority, a friend—not just a parent—who thinks change can happen.

I tear off the sheet and he takes it in his left hand and stares at it. I stand up and say "Let's get moving, Walker," and go a few paces down the path and turn. But he doesn't move. He's still reading and thinking, trying to see, as any reader does, how words can illuminate his darkness.

He looks terrific. Sitting there deep in thought, he strikes me as a much handsomer version of myself at that age. He's leaning forward with his back straight, elbows on his knees, hands close together holding the two lists. He frowns at the mystery in front of him: life as it is in his right hand and life as he'd like it to be in his left. A long moment goes by, and weekend athletes pass. Then—surprise!— his face brightens and he springs to his feet, faces me, and bounces in place on the tips of his toes, waving the two sheets of paper in his hands. He raises his eyes skyward in the astonished-at-life, delighted way he does. "Ah, ah AHHH!" he shouts, startling a middle-aged runner, who veers off the path and gives him a "What the…?" look.

Then, with a grin, Walker starts to race toward me. I turn and run alongside him with a near-identical grin on my own face. I wonder, *How does he do it?* He seems to extract exuberance from the very air he breathes.

On this day, as on so many days, the way life is and the way life should be are really the same thing.

17 $\frac{95}{}$